TORT LIABILITY FOR HUMAN RIGHTS ABUSES

Advancing a bold theory of the relevance of tort law in the fight against human rights abuses, celebrated US law professor George Fletcher here challenges the community of international lawyers to think again about how they can use the Alien Tort Statute. Beginning with an historical analysis, Fletcher shows how tort and criminal law originally evolved to deal with similar problems, how tort came to be seen as primarily concerned with negligence, and how the Alien Tort Statute has helped establish the importance of tort law in international cases. In a series of cases starting with *Filartiga* and culminating most recently in *Sosa*, Fletcher shows how torture cases led to the reawakening of the Alien Tort Statute, changing US law and giving legal practitioners a tool with which to assist victims of torture and other extreme human rights abuses. This leads to an examination of Agent Orange and the possible commission of war crimes in the course of its utilisation, and the theory of liability for aiding and abetting the US military and other military forces when they commit war crimes. The book concludes by looking at the cutting-edge cases in this area, particularly those involving liability for funding terrorism, and the remedies available, particularly the potential offered by the compensation chamber in the International Criminal Court.

D1553799

Tort Liability for Human Rights Abuses

George P Fletcher

·HART·
PUBLISHING

OXFORD AND PORTLAND, OREGON
2008

Published in North America (US and Canada) by
Hart Publishing
c/o International Specialized Book Services
920 NE 58th Avenue, Suite 300
Portland, OR 97213-3786
USA
Tel: +1 503 287 3093 or toll-free: (1) 800 944 6190
Fax: +1 503 280 8832
E-mail: orders@isbs.com
Website: http://www.isbs.com

Hart Publishing Ltd, 16C Worcester Place, Oxford, OX1 2JW
Telephone: +44 (0)1865 517530 Fax: +44 (0)1865 510710
E-mail: mail@hartpub.co.uk
Website: http://www.hartpub.co.uk

British Library Cataloguing in Publication Data
Data Available

ISBN: 978-1-84113-794-0

Typeset by Compuscript Ltd, Shannon
Printed and bound in Great Britain by
TJ International Ltd, Padstow, Cornwall

For Francisco,
the beloved father of Brachah

Contents

Introduction

The New Rights

Since World War II a great conceptual transformation has occurred in the way politicians and lawyers think about individual rights against governments. In the 1930s and 1940s these rights were called civil rights and civil liberties. The US Supreme Court was the centre of this development. The justices engaged far-reaching issues of free speech and freedom of the press, the right to a fair trial, and the suppression of racial discrimination. The struggles for these constitutional rights were fought specifically under the banner of 'civil rights' and 'civil liberties'.

1. RIGHTS FOR HUMANS

With the United Nations Charter of 26 June 1945 and the Universal Declaration of Human Rights, passed by the newly born General Assembly on 10 December 1948, a new language came into focus—the idiom of *human* rights.[1] The idiom changed but the substance did not. The same rights that American constitutional lawyers had fought for since the enactment of the Bill of Rights in 1891 had taken on new connotations. They were universal rights, belonging to everyone—not because they were American or subject to the jurisdiction of the American states, but just because they attached to every human being. After the Civil War, the Fourteenth Amendment of the US Constitution recognised that the right to equal protection of the laws accrued to everyone simply because they were 'persons' within the jurisdiction of a state. No state could discriminate against human beings under its power nor could it deprive of them of life, liberty, or property without due process of

---

[1] The UN Charter refers to 'human rights' several times. See Preamble, and Arts 1, 55, and 76.

law. After World War II the American idea became the universal idea. Under the inspiration of Eleanor Roosevelt and the United Nations, the notion of rights based on personhood became applicable to the world.

But because these newly expressed human rights were part of international law—not domestic law—there was a problem. There was no court available to enforce them. The International Court of Justice, founded in 1945, had its jurisdiction limited to lawsuits brought by states against states. This was the pattern of international law. States could sue states, but individuals had no direct access to court to complain of the violation of their rights.

A low expectation of enforcement has a positive side. When drafters know that the norms of a treaty are likely to be admired but not directly applied, they are free to incorporate more grandiose ambitions in their treaties. The Declaration of Independence provides us with an early guide to this style of far-reaching rhetoric. 'All men are created equal. They are endowed by their creator with unalienable rights, among these are life, liberty, and the pursuit of happiness.' This is inspiring language. We find similar examples in the post-World War II treaties on human rights.

The purpose of the Universal Declaration of Human Rights was to educate, to provide goals for evolving societies, to represent ideals, but not to provide the rule of decision in disputed cases. A good example is Article 6: 'Everyone has the right to recognition everywhere as a person before the law.' No one would disagree with this, as no one would disagree that all men have the fundamental right to the pursuit of happiness. But if these aspirations are disputed in concrete cases, they are not norms for courts to apply to fine-tune the law.

This quality of wishful thinking comes through most clearly in the recognition of the so-called social rights, the affirmative entitlements to certain treatment from the government. These include the right to work, free choice of employment, a right to payment or 'an existence worthy of human dignity' (all in Article 23 of the Universal Declaration), the right to rest and leisure (Article 24 of the same), the right to education (Article 26 of the same), and many more. These are worthy goals but hardly the basis for a body of law designed to correct case by case the injustices of the world.

The two lasting problems of the Universal Declaration and subsequent treaties on human rights, then, are the means of enforcement and the definition of precise standards for courts to invoke in litigating disputes. The two phenomena are obviously connected. When immediate action by the courts and governmental agencies is not expected we have more room to express our dreams for a better society.

At the same time, other critical events in the post-World-War-II period were bringing home the idea that individuals—not only states—had both rights and duties under international law. The Nuremberg proceedings provided an arena for establishing the individual criminal responsibility of the leaders of the Nazi regime, and analogous courts in the Far East indicted and convicted the Japanese warlords. At the heart of the Nuremberg proceedings was the idea that each government was responsible under international law not only to the citizens of other countries but to the persons living within their own borders. In order to achieve this ideal, international law had to recreate the principle underlying the US Fourteenth Amendment, namely the idea that no state could deprive any person of life, liberty, or property without due process of law. The genocide of German Jews was obviously a violation of this principle, but not a violation recognised under traditional principles of state-to-state responsibility. A new idea was necessary, and the prosecutors found this idea in the newly coined term 'crime against humanity'—that is, against human beings. Not only were the interests of states protected under international law but each human being in the world was protected against the commission of crimes against humanity.

Note the distinction between these two senses of human rights under international law. One bears resemblance to the bearing of rights under constitutional regimes. The other is the right to be held responsible for crimes committed against others. The first is about the dignity of being a person endowed with rights, the second about the dignity of being a person treated as capable of wilfully and responsibly committing evil.

Another important innovation of the time took place in a US military tribunal set up to try the alleged war crimes of a Japanese General named Tomoyuki Yamashita who allegedly failed to supervise his troops properly as they went on a rampage and slaughtered civilians in the Philippines. The US Supreme Court invented a new crime known as command responsibility. If a commander negligently fails to supervise his troops in the field, he is a guilty of one of the most serious war crimes. Yamashita was sentenced to death.[2] The principle born in this case, now firmly established, was used frequently in the International Criminal Tribunal for the former Yugoslavia (ICTY) and codified in the Rome Statute establishing the International Criminal Court (ICC).[3]

Thus the protection of human rights has three dimensions: the securing of rights in the conventional constitutional sense; the protection of all victims, not only those who are citizens of foreign states; and the necessity to stand trial for crimes committed against humanity. The creation of these aspects to human rights testifies to the judicial creativity resulting from the vast abuses of human dignity in World War II.

The new discourse of human rights looked forward to a new world 'scourged of war',[4] committed to preventing the same crimes from occurring again. Newly established international tribunals undertook to punish the crimes connected to the war (in practice, those committed by the enemy). Yet no one spoke about using the tort remedy either for the purpose of achieving justice relative to the past or to secure the protection of individual rights in the future. That would come later.

2. UNIVERSAL JURISDICTION

The carving out of the individual as the subject of international law dovetailed with another major shift in attitudes towards jurisdiction or the power of courts to decide criminal cases. The traditional rule is that courts have jurisdiction over crimes committed on their national territory—or, at the most, by nationals of the country. But the post-war criminal tribunals were interested not in geography, but in functional results. They wanted to prosecute those guilty of war crimes and crimes against humanity regardless where the crimes occurred. The theory was that if the crimes occurred against all of humanity, then the representatives of humanity—in this case, the international community—should be able to prosecute these crimes wherever they occurred.

---

[2] *In re Yamashita*, 327 US 1 (1946).
[3] See Rome Statute, Art 28.
[4] Adapted from the United Nations Charter, Preamble.

The new theory was called universal jurisdiction. As international law came to focus on individuals in place of states, the courts too disregarded the limitations of national identity. They spoke in the name of the international community and they claimed jurisdiction regardless of where they were and where the crimes were committed.

The idea had venerable roots—or at least it was so argued. The leading example was always piracy. Robbery on the high seas has no natural home and therefore if any state has authority to prosecute pirates, all have the same claim. Beginning roughly in Warsaw in 1927, a number of international groups recommended universal jurisdiction over a series of offences beyond piracy, for example for slave trading, a condemned practice touching upon many states. Under the National Socialist government, the Germans enthusiastically pursued the idea of universal jurisdiction by adopting a new provision of the criminal code that punishes a pot-pourri of offences, including some odd ones such as disseminating obscene materials and the fraudulent receipt of subsidies.[5] Many of these provisions originated in the proposals made in Warsaw, but there were no apparent criteria for including some offences and not others. After World War II, the idea of universal jurisdiction drew largely on the model of the Nuremberg trials and grounded itself in the evil of the offence and the offender. The Genocide Convention of 1948 called upon all signatories to enact a crime of genocide but still recommends that jurisdiction be limited to the territory of the crime and to international courts to which member states had conceded jurisdiction.[6] For a long period of time the Germans retained their list of universally prosecuted offences drawn from the Nationalist Socialist period and added new offences based on the Nuremberg principle of evil that ought to be prosecuted by all civilised peoples. Genocide eventually replaced piracy as the paradigm offence in the European conception of universal jurisdiction.[7] The new emphasis on evil had an obvious purpose—to counteract the risk that evil culprits would flee to foreign ports and escape prosecution.

---

[5] StGB, Art 6.

[6] Genocide Convention of 1948, Art 6.

[7] Germany passed the *Völkerstrafgesetzbuch* in June 2002, granting universal jurisdiction over genocide. Spain granted its courts jurisdiction over 'crimes which, under international treaties or conventions, are required to be prosecuted' in 1985. The UK claims universal jurisdiction over all genocidal acts committed after the enactment of the Rome Statute.

The risk of impunity for wrongdoers would not be significant if all the states in the world could be counted on both to extradite suspects and to prosecute their nationals or those who commit crimes on their territories. Suspicion towards rogue states has led many European powers to believe that they must assert universal jurisdiction over the crimes equivalent in evil to those prosecuted in special tribunals established in the aftermath of Auschwitz.

The Geneva Conventions of 1949 urged all states to adopt legislation to prosecute grave breaches of the Convention, wherever they occurred.[8] The list is specific:

(1) wilful killing, torture or inhuman treatment, including biological experiments;
(2) wilfully causing great suffering or serious injury to body or health;
(3) compelling a prisoner of war to serve in the forces of the hostile power; or
(4) wilfully depriving a prisoner of war of the rights of fair and regular trial prescribed in this Convention.

Although Americans played the leading role in organising post-World War II proceedings, they balked at the recommendation of the Geneva Conventions. They did not adopt conforming legislation until 1996, and even then the offence was limited to wrongful actions committed by or against Americans or members of the US armed forces.[9]

It is not clear why Americans objected to the culmination of the trend they initiated at Nuremberg. There might be arguments against universal jurisdiction but, so far as I know, American policy-makers never articulated very convincing objections.[10]

The fear—often voiced—that other countries will file false charges against American peacekeepers abroad is not on point, for

---

[8] 1949 Third Geneva Conventions, Art 130.
[9] 18 USC 2441.
[10] I have made some of these points in 'Against Universal Jurisdiction' (2003) 1 *Journal of International Criminal Justice* 579. Compare William W Burke-White, who, with the help of Ruth Wedgewood, makes a normative argument against universal jurisdiction, but then promotes the idea of regional jurisdiction over human rights violations in 'Regionalization of International Criminal Law Enforcement: A Preliminary Exploration' (2003) 38 *Texas International Law Journal* 729.

these states can claim jurisdiction based on the territory where the offence is committed, whether we concur or not.[11] Other common law countries have eagerly pursued the policies both of asserting universal jurisdiction and of supporting the ICC.[12]

In another bold gesture the Geneva Conventions established a principle of liability that would apply even to states and sub-state organisations engaged in armed conflicts that were not international in nature—which presumably meant of an internal nature. These principles applied to everyone as though they were customary international law adopted by the practice of nations. Called 'Common Article 3', because it appears in all four of the Conventions, the list of offences is remarkably like the grave breaches:

(a) violence to life and person, in particular murder of all kinds, mutilation, cruel treatment and torture;
(b) the taking of hostages;
(c) outrages upon personal dignity, in particular, humiliating and degrading treatment;
(d) the passing of sentences and the carrying out of executions without previous judgment pronounced by a regularly constituted court affording all the judicial guarantees which are recognised as indispensable by civilised peoples.

The US Supreme Court recently applied this provision in order to strike down military commissions created by President Bush because they violated the 'judicial guarantees which are recognised as indispensable by civilised peoples'.[13] American prosecutors cannot indict directly on the basis of the defined grave breaches of Common Article 3 because crimes subject to punishment in US courts must be defined as crime by local legislation before they can be prosecuted. Yet the Geneva Conventions stand for general principles of law that the courts could invoke to block military commissions and other institutions that deny defendants their basic rights of due process.[14]

---

[11] Rome Statute, Art 12(2)(a).
[12] The UK passed the International Criminal Court Act 2001, which details the responsibilities of state officials to support the ICC.
[13] *Hamdan v Rumsfeld*, 548 US 557 (2006).
[14] Common Art 3 provides a source of fundamental rights when the court wishes to avoid applying the Constitution to offshore places of detention, such as Guantanamo Bay.

In the context of these post-war flirtations with international principles of human rights, one uniquely American institution stands out and deserves our attention. This is the Alien Torts Statute, which was adopted immediately after another war—one fought over two hundred years ago, the American War of Independence. As soon as the country constituted itself in a federal government based on the Constitution that went into force in 1789, the first Congress adopted a Judiciary Act that created the lower federal courts and defined their jurisdiction. This venerable piece of legislation, called the First Judiciary Act, has acquired near-constitutional status. We will find this statute coming up over and over again in the history and development of US law.

One of its provisions was quiescent—nearly forgotten for two hundred years. In section 9 of the Act Congress vested 'cognizance' or jurisdiction in the new federal courts 'concurrent with the courts of the several States, or the circuit courts, as the case may be, of all causes where an alien sues for a tort only in violation of the law of nations or of a treaty of the United States'.[15] Since then this language has remained a part of the federal legislative landscape. In its currently edited form, it provides that 'the district courts shall have original jurisdiction of any civil action by an alien for a tort only, committed in violation of the law of nations or a treaty of the United States'.[16] For years this statute was known as the Alien Torts Claims Act, or the ATCA, also known as the Alien Torts Statute, or the ATS.[17]

This provision in the First Judiciary Act has created a unique version of universal jurisdiction—one that you would never expect to find in the United States. Presumably, in 1789, no one referred to the ATCA as an instance of universal jurisdiction. In fact, the term 'universal jurisdiction' was probably unknown at the time. Even today, it would be unusual to refer to the ATCA as an instance of universal jurisdiction, largely because the scholars who write about the latter topic limit their focus to criminal law. And yet today, so

[15] Act of Sept 24, 1789, ch 20, § 9(b), 1 Stat 79 n 10.
[16] 28 USC § 1350.
[17] The latter term entered the law in the Supreme Court's major pronouncement on the meaning of the ATCA, *Sosa v Alvarez-Machain*, 542 US 692 (2004) [hereafter cited as *Sosa* with page references to this citation]. Since I view the history and meaning as broader than *Sosa* opinion, I retain the traditional label.

far as we are concerned about finding a forum to correct the evil of human rights abuses, the ATCA is probably the most effective instrument available in the world. This is a major claim, and it will take me some time to make good on it.

The ATCA evolved from a footnote to the Judiciary Statute of 1789 into an institution recognised in 1980 as a primary arena for litigating human rights. This is an extraordinary story of legal adaptation, one that would not have been possible without the concurrent events we have described in the aftermath of World War II. Virtually all of this development has occurred in the last 25 years.[18] The adaptation of the ATCA enables us to understand how the United States could support universal jurisdiction in Nuremberg and yet shy away from current European proposals to use universal jurisdiction to prosecute egregious crimes wherever they have occurred. The preference for tort law over criminal law is largely an American story.

As compared to jurists in Europe, Asia, and Latin America—indeed just about everywhere in the world—US human rights lawyers have many reasons to think 'tort' instead of 'crime'. Tort law is based on private incentives rather the decisions of a governmental bureaucracy. This suits the American temperament for taking private action—even seeking private revenge—rather than relying on government bureaucracy do it for them. As I have shown elsewhere,[19] Europeans may say that the criminal sanction is the *ultima ratio*, the measure of last resort, but in fact they use it more often than do Americans to solve the problems of pollution and dangerous products, even minor problems of fraud and deceit.[20]

What makes the tort remedy so attractive in the United States? The answer is very simple—money. The combination of the jury system and the contingency fee means that tort awards are large and that tort lawyers can receive monetary rewards far in excess of their hourly fee. And let us not forget that we have in mind cases of

[18] *Filartiga v Pena-Irala*, 630 F2d 876 (2d Cir 1980).
[19] George P Fletcher, *The Grammar of Criminal Law: American, Comparative, International* (New York, Oxford University Press, 2007) 127 [hereafter cited as *The Grammar*].
[20] On the rather curious attitude of the European Community towards the crime of subsidy fraud as a basis for establishing a Union-wide system of criminal law, see my article 'Parochial versus Universal Criminal Law' (2005) 3 *Journal of International Criminal Justice* 20.

malicious behaviour depriving others of their human rights: these inevitably invite punitive damage awards far in excess of compensatory damages. No other country offers all these incentives to litigate in tort rather than sit and wait for the state to pay for a criminal prosecution. Of course, the lawyers must invest resources in the development of the case and they risk losing their stake, but, still, the opportunities are enticing. The lawyers can do well and do good for the world at the same time. The tort remedy—coupled with the jury system and the contingency fee and punitive damages—creates a powerful system of incentives for litigating human rights abuses.

We have indirectly mentioned two of the factors that influenced the adoption of the original 1789 ATCA. As the story is often told,[21] one purpose of the statute was to provide a private remedy easily accessible to foreigners that would enable them, without reliance on the state governments or federal officials, to receive redress for private wrongs—invasions of their privacy or person. A couple of incidents in the early days of the Republic convinced the founders that a private remedy was necessary to avoid the risk that a foreigner's suffering a personal grievance might escalate into a breakdown of international relations, bringing with it the risk of war.

The most dramatic incident was the Marbois affair. A Frenchman named Chevalier de Longchamps attacked the secretary of the French legation, Francis Marbois, on a public street in Philadelphia. The incident generated a diplomatic flap, largely because the Continental Congress could do nothing to satisfy the French. It had neither the authority to prosecute nor the capacity to recommend an alternative civil remedy. The most the Continental Congress could do was to urge Pennsylvania to prosecute, which the local authorities eventually did in the *Longchamps* case.[22] The court convicting and sentencing Longchamps discussed the assault against the ambassador in terms that should make us realise how serious the matter was at the time:

> The person of a public minister is sacred and inviolable. Whoever offers any violence to him, not only affronts the Sovereign he represents, but

---

[21] The leading article, cited often by the court in the *Sosa* opinion, is William Casto, 'The Federal Courts' Protective Jurisdiction Over Torts Committed in Violation of the Law of Nations' (1986) 18 *Connecticut Law Review* 467.

[22] *Respublica v Longchamps*, 1 US 111 (Philadelphia Court of Oyer and Terminer, 1784).

also hurts the common safety and well-being of nations;—he is guilty of a crime against the whole world.[23]

This is the way we speak today about crimes against humanity.

In pronouncing sentence the judge emphasised that the purpose of the prosecution was to 'preserve the honor of the State, and maintain peace with our great and good Ally and the whole world'.[24] Another incident in New York during the Constitutional Convention reminded the constitutional drafters of the urgency of the matter. A local constable entered the home of the Dutch ambassador in clear violation of the latter's immunity. The Continental Congress could do nothing but await the action of the New York authorities (who did finally convict the constable).[25] One response to the necessity of providing a fast remedy in these minor matters was recognition in the Constitution of the original jurisdiction in the Supreme Court over 'all Cases affecting Ambassadors, other public Ministers and Consuls'.[26] The other response was the enactment of the ATCA in the Judiciary Act of 1789.

The Constitution could have provided for federal criminal jurisdiction in cases bearing on foreign affairs, but there was considerable wisdom in leaving these matters to the private sphere. Tort suits are in the hands of the victim. An aggrieved alien can bring suit immediately. There is no need for a central authority, powerless to act, to urge, to inveigle, or to plead for prosecution by state officials. While there were still options of private prosecution in 1789, the time would come soon in which prosecutors would exercise non-reviewable discretion over their cases.[27] The great advantage of tort suits is that no victim can complain against the state that it has stood silently by while someone within its jurisdiction has violated of the law of nations.

It would be a stretch to imagine that the drafters of the Judiciary Act had their minds set on the modern concept of universal jurisdiction, but an episode in 1794 reminded American lawyers of

---

[23] *Ibid* at 116.
[24] *Ibid* at 117.
[25] See Casto, above n 21, at 472.
[26] US Constitution, Art III, § 2.
[27] See *Brack v Wells*, 184 Md 86, 40 A2d 319 (1944), in which the Court of Appeals for Maryland refused to issue a writ of mandamus to force a prosecutor to bring charges.

the inherent limitations of criminal jurisdiction. An American slave trader led a French band in sacking the British territory of Sierra Leone. The British Ambassador protested the role of the American slave trader as a violation of American neutrality. Attorney General William Bradford wrote an official opinion declaring the American's act to be criminal but beyond the territorial jurisdiction of the United States. Nonetheless, he wrote that, under the ATCA, the 'company or individuals who have been injured by these acts have a remedy by a civil suit in the courts of the United States'.[28] Bradford realised that tort suits—but not criminal prosecution—could easily be abstracted from the foreign territory where the incident occurred and subject to adjudication in the United States.

As of the late eighteenth century, criminal cases were understood to be local, but tort cases were transitory. They were based on 'transitory causes of action', which meant that they could be litigated in any place where the parties could establish personal jurisdiction. The dispute was between the two parties and it travelled with them. The situation in criminal law was then and has remained different. Traditional crime is linked to the community where it occurs. The victims are part of the landscape. They are often interred in the local cemetery. As the story of Cain and Abel reminds us, the victim's blood cries up from the ground.[29] Perhaps this explains why the Sixth Amendment guarantees criminal defendants a trial 'by an impartial jury of the State and district wherein the crime shall have been committed'.

The transitory cause of action should be regarded as the proper beginning of universal jurisdiction. In private disputes the idea is that the fight is personal and bilateral. The community where the tort or contract occurred has no stake in adjudicating the case. In normal criminal cases, the situation is reversed. In fact the community is critically involved and thus we find the rule about localising jury trials. Crimes are violations of the local public interest as well as of private interests.

International criminal law has given a unique spin to the idea of community. At the level of egregious human rights violations, the

---

[28] Opinion of William Bradford, 1 Opinions of the Attorney General (1795) at 57.
[29] Genesis 4:10.

relevant framework is the entire community of nations—or so it is said. Crimes against humanity—an invention of the international legal order—supposedly means that all of humanity can claim to be the relevant community. This argument can justify centralisation of prosecution in an international criminal court but it is with some difficulty that it can also justify the decentralisation of international authority to the point that every nation is entitled to speak for humanity.

If we compare the two, then, universality in tort disputes seems more plausible than universality in criminal cases. Tort disputes are abstracted from the *locus delicti*. Even the traditional rule that tort disputes are governed by the *lex loci delicti* is no longer taken for granted. Brainerd Currie's theory of conflicts of law hammered the final nail in the coffin of territoriality. If two New Yorkers have an accident in Ontario, Currie—with the courts following him—would apply the law of New York and not the law of Ontario.[30]

The very existence of the field called 'conflicts of law' testifies to the radical difference between the transitory nature of private disputes and the localised, rooted nature of criminal prosecutions. In criminal cases, almost always, jurisdiction determines the choice of law. Whether a crime has been committed, whether it is justified, when the defendant is culpable—these are determined by the law of the forum. There is no room for a methodology of choice of law that would result in the application of foreign law. It seems obvious that tort disputes can be abstracted from geography in a way in which criminal cases cannot be. Therefore, we should conclude that universal jurisdiction is a more compelling institution in tort law than it is in criminal law.

The legal culture as a whole has adapted better to transitory causes of action in private disputes than it has to the assertion of universality in criminal jurisdiction. The danger in any system that permits litigation in more than one court is that if the defendant wins in one court, the victim can seek justice in another court. In order to avoid repeated litigation of the same issue, civil parties are protected by a strong rule of *res judicata*, which means once a dispute is decided it should not be addressed anew in other courts.

---

[30] Brainerd Currie, 'The Disinterested Third State' (1963) 28 *Law & Contemporary Problems* 754 at 757.

The rule might be mandatory, as it is under the Full Faith and Credit Clause of the US Constitution or the analogous rule of the European Union. Or it might be extended as a matter of comity, as among independent states. In private litigation, the principle of mutual respect governs the impact of judicial decisions on other courts around the world.

You would expect the same thing to be true in criminal cases. Avoidance of double jeopardy is widely recognised as a constitutional right (in a way that the *res judicata* is not explicitly so recognised). But in fact the right is treated as limited to recurrent prosecution within a single jurisdiction. There is no general norm of international law precluding a different sovereign from initiating a new prosecution. If a person is acquitted of war crimes in France or Germany, nothing precludes prosecution in Canada for the same offence.[31] Even in the United States, the double jeopardy clause is interpreted to permit multiple prosecutions in technically separate jurisdictions. A state prosecution does not preclude a federal prosecution,[32] and if a crime occurs in two states, both states are entitled to prosecute, one after the other.[33] None of this is very fair. One explanation is that in the United States, the prosecution cannot appeal an acquittal (unlike Continental jurisdictions and some common law systems, for example Canada[34]). They are compensated, functionally, for this deprivation by having the option of a federal prosecution after an acquittal in state court.

In the final analysis, then, universal jurisdiction under the ATCA should be seen as a perfectly sensible institution—at least as plausible as the widely advocated institution of universal criminal jurisdiction as a means of counteracting human rights abuses. Some readers might baulk at this interpretation of the ATCA. They

---

[31] *R v Finta* [1994] 1 SCR 701.

[32] Officer Lawrence Powell and Sergeant Stacey Koon were convicted by a federal court for the beating of Rodney King. This federal court conviction occurred after the two LA policemen were acquitted by a California state trial that led to the famous LA riots of 1992. This conviction was appealed on sentencing issues to the Supreme Court but the double jeopardy issue was so settled in US law that it was not even raised in the appeal: *Koon v United States* 116 S Ct 2035.

[33] *Heath v Alabama*, 106 S Ct 433 at 437–8.

[34] In accordance with s 676 of the Canadian Criminal Code, the prosecutor can appeal on questions of law or of sentences not mandated by statute.

would mention the limitation of serving process—the necessity of 'tagging' the defendant in the jurisdiction of the court by serving papers on him. To be precise, the subject we have been discussing so far is in fact only part of the issue of jurisdiction—properly called 'subject-matter jurisdiction': the jurisdiction over the claim as it is defined by who did what, when, where, and perhaps why. The question remains open as to how the court acquires jurisdiction over the person of the criminal suspect.

3. ACQUIRING JURISDICTION OVER THE PERSON

In personam jurisdiction is totally independent of subject-matter jurisdiction, both in criminal and in tort cases. The common law of crime employs a simple principle for determining when the court acquires jurisdiction over the person of the defendant. In criminal cases, the body must appear before the court. The presence of the defendant establishes the necessary link between the sovereign power of the state and the person of the defendant. If the sovereign has the defendant in court, it can judge him—even if he thereafter escapes from the jurisdiction. The rule is so simple that nothing else matters. If the defendant is in court, no one asks how he or she got there.

Wilful blindness towards the procedures prior to the defendant's appearance in court have some admittedly unsatisfying implications. For example, it does not matter whether the defendant was tricked into coming into court or whether he was kidnapped and forced to appear. As was known from the famous *Eichmann*[35] and *Noriega*[36] cases, kidnapping is one of the procedures used to establish *in personam* jurisdiction of the court over the body of the accused. One can understand the objections of international lawyers against a system of jurisdiction that turns a blind eye to the practice of kidnapping.[37]

In common-law private law cases, the analogue to having the body present in court is the symbolic act of acquiring control of the

---

[35] *Attorney General v Adolph Eichmann*, 36 *Israel Law Reports* 5 (1961).
[36] *United States v Noriega*, 683 F Supp 1373 (1988).
[37] Although the US Supreme Court accepted the practice as constitutional in: *Kerr v Illinois*, 119 US 436 (1986).

defendant's body by serving process on the defendant within the jurisdiction of the court. Basically this means that a process-server must locate the person within the jurisdiction, verify his or her identity, and place the papers in his or her possession, preferably with a photographer present. Traditionally, service by registered mail or publication in a newspaper was not sufficient.[38] Admittedly there has been some deviation from the rule in special cases, with the imprimatur of a court order, but the basic principle of service on the person still holds.

In an amusing example of this procedure, Radovan Karadžić visited new York to speak at the United Nations about the conditions of the Bosnian Serbs.[39] One of his alleged victims tried to serve process on him at the UN. but was not able to do so because Karadžić enjoyed immunity from service when he was in the physical territory of the UN and in the course of transport back and forth to the UN buildings. But the plaintiffs found a loophole. Karadžić had no immunity at the Inter-Continental Hotel where he was staying and therefore the process-server could reach him there. This led to the famous ATCA precedent in the case of *Kadic v Karadžić*, decided by the Second Circuit—a case discussed later.[40] The rituals of serving process may seem quaint to European lawyers but they represent a major advance over the rather brutal system of the criminal courts, which encourages kidnapping and forcible appearance before the court.

The problem in Continental jurisprudence is finding out exactly what takes the place of service of process in the common law system. Sometimes civilian systems permit the posting of a notice of the trial at the District Attorney's Office, and this is supposedly sufficient to acquire jurisdiction over the person of the defendant. But this procedure could hardly be fair in a case of universal jurisdiction, where the defendant has no reason to keep informed of notices posted in countries with which he has had no personal relationship. It is not surprising, then, that advocates of universal jurisdiction require a compromise that comes close to the principle of service of process, namely that the defendant must have entered the territory

---

[38] *Pennoyer v Neff*, 95 US 714 (1877).
[39] *Kadic v Karadžić*, 70 F3d 232, 245 (2d Cir 1995).
[40] *Ibid*. See further discussion in ch 5, pp 127–8.

of the prosecuting state.[41] The German courts speak about 'significant contacts' with the forum, which is a term either borrowed from or accidentally similar to a term popular in the common law of jurisdiction in civil cases.[42] The Rome Statute offers no illumination whatsoever about this procedural requirement.

Suffice it to say that the European mindset about these matters differs fundamentally from the American conceptions of jurisdiction. For example, some European countries are willing to take seriously the possibility of trials in absentia—that is, trials where the defendant has never set foot in the courtroom.[43] This would be unthinkable in the common law tradition. A full analysis of the European analogue to American principles of jurisdiction over the person is beyond our ken, and I would guess is not yet available in the literature.[44] For the purpose of our study, however, we need only note that the problem of universal jurisdiction falls into two categories, which we document in the table below:

	Subject-matter Jurisdiction	Jurisdiction over the Person
Common law torts	Universal jurisdiction under the ATCA	Service of process
Continental criminal case	Universal jurisdiction in egregious criminal cases	Analogues uncertain— possible trial in absentia

4. THE BASIC ELEMENTS OF THE ATCA

With this background in the principles of private law and criminal law, we can take a closer look at the component parts of the ATCA.

[41] See the Federal Supreme Court in the case of *Nicola Jorgic*, 30 April 1999. According to the statute adopted in 2002, however, Germany appears not to require presence in the state (§ 1 of the German Code of Crimes against International Law); however, the prosecutor has discretion not to prosecute cases in which presence is not anticipated (see Code of Criminal Procedure, § 153f, (2), No 2).

[42] *International Shoe v State of Washington*, 326 US 310 (1945).

[43] See the Reuters report on the threat by the Italian government to prosecute 22 American CIA agents in absentia, 13 February 2006, http://www.craigmurray.org.uk/archives/2006/02/italy_may_put_c.htm.

[44] Canada is an interesting case. It adopts universal jurisdiction(see s 8 of the Crimes against Humanity and War Crimes Act 2000),and it might retain the rule that jurisdiction is achieved by taking possession over the body of the defendant.

Only about half a dozen words matter in the venerable 1789 Statute, Each of them requires some reflection and analysis.

(1) 'By an alien'. Only aliens can claim federal jurisdiction for torts in violation of the law of nations. Nothing is said about the nationality of the defendant, whether he or she must also be an alien or must be a national or resident of the United States. Numerous puzzles arise.

First, according to the Constitution, Article III, section 2, clause 1, the judicial power of the federal courts is limited to nine subdivisions, eight of which have nothing to do with aliens or foreign states. The ninth subdivision provides that the courts shall have jurisdiction in all cases 'between a State, or the Citizens thereof, and foreign States, Citizens or Subjects'. These are forms of the diversity model, which in an earlier clause provides for jurisdiction in all cases 'between citizens of different states'. The possibilities of diversity arising from subdivision 9 are these:

(1) a state vs a foreign state;
(2) a state vs citizens of a foreign state;
(3) a state vs subjects of a foreign state;
(4) citizens of a state vs a foreign state;
(5) citizens of a state vs citizens of a foreign state;
(6) citizens of a state vs subjects of a foreign state.

Before we draw any inferences from the structure laid out above, we should be clear about a few of the terms. 'State' refers to a state of the United States. 'Foreign state' refers to a state outside of the United States. 'Citizens of a state' refers to US citizens, and 'subjects of a foreign state' refers to aliens. Now the general structure of subdivision 9 comes in focus. On one side you have US citizens or US states, and on the other side, you have aliens or foreign entities.

The implication is that by the intent of the framers, the jurisdiction of the ATCA should have been limited to suits by aliens in tort only against Americans or US states. But this is an incongruous interpretation from the very outset. Recall that the Marbois affair, which provides one of the models for the ATCA, occurred between two Frenchmen. When the case went to trial, the court articulated one of the basic policies behind the ATCA, namely that the assault upon the French ambassador 'affronts the Sovereign he represents, but also hurts the common safety and well-being of nations;—he is guilty of a crime against the whole world'.[45] In order to correct offence of this sort and thus preserve the peace, Congress instituted the alien tort remedy. Of course, the Marbois affair did occur on the territory of the United States. This gave the United States an interest in resolving the dispute and therefore it was plausible to suggest that if the United States provided no relief, the flap might escalate into an international incident. Unfortunately, territory is not a relevant factor in the constitutional definition of jurisdiction. When the incident occurs outside the United States it might make sense, therefore, to require the defendant to be a US citizen.

The fact is that the courts have ignored this constitutional problem. After 1875, when Congress recognised a general category of cases 'arising under federal law',[46] the argument was that the suits of one alien against another could be justified under the latter category. But this raises another problem that the courts have hoped to avoid, namely whether the ATCA states a substantive cause of action. This is a very subtle issue that lends itself to diverse interpretations. It is not clear what a substantive cause of action is and how an alien could recover in tort for violation of the law of nations without triggering liability under a substantive cause of action. But it is better for now that we leave these problems to one side. The discussion is plagued by ambiguities about the meanings of it critical terms, for example the meaning of 'arising under', of 'violations of international law', and of 'a substantive cause of action'. Yet in 2004, when the Supreme Court took up the ATCA for the first time in its 215-year history, the court ruled that the ATCA does not provide a substantive cause of action, and yet the court had no doubts about the constitutionality of any of the precedents granting recovery for violations of the law of nations. The Supreme Court case—*Sosa v Alvarez-Machain*[47]—will later concern us in detail but for now we rely on it as authority to put aside some nagging constitutional questions about the use of the ATCA to enable aliens to sue other aliens for violations of international law that occurred in their home countries.[48]

---

[45] See above n 22.
[46] 28 USC § 1331.
[47] 542 US 692 (2004).
[48] See the discussion below of *Filartiga v Pena-Irala*, above n 18, which used the 'arising under' factor solely to establish jurisdiction, not to justify the creation of a new cause of action.

History has overtaken theory. In the contemporary resurgence of the Alien Tort Statute—in its modern use as an instrument for correcting human rights abuses—it is assumed that aliens may sue other aliens in federal court, provided they serve process on them in US territory. The first big case, already mentioned, was that of a Paraguayan suing a fellow Paraguayan in New York for torture committed in Paraguay (*Filartiga*).[49] The jurisdiction of one alien suing another was, and still is, assumed to be constitutional.[50] There would be no problem in an alien's suing another alien in state court for a tort that occurred abroad. The ATCA recognises that these cases can be tried in federal court as well, provided there is a violation of the law of nations. This, then, is the universal side of the ATCA, and for our purposes, this is the aspect of the statute that has enabled it to function as an instrument for establishing and correcting major human rights abuses.

It is worth noting another constitutional issue in the ATCA that, I dare say, no one has discussed. How do we justify granting only to aliens the power to bring lawsuits to correct human rights abuses? Is this a kind of affirmative action for aliens before its time? Suppose both an American and a Paraguayan are tortured in Paraguay. The police chief responsible later comes on a visit to the United States. The Paraguayan sues under the ATCA. What does the American do? She can bring an ordinary tort action in state court against the police chief (the Paraguayan can do this too). She can also bring a suit in federal court under the diversity jurisdiction granted for suits by citizens against citizens of foreign states.[51] If there is any dispute about liability for torture, the American Victims Torture Act of 1991 makes it more than clear that any American can recover for the kind of tort litigated in *Filartiga*.[52] It is not obvious, however, if recovery is dubious both in tort law and in international law, whether the ATCA will create an opportunity

---

[49] *Filartiga v Pena-Irala*, above n 18.

[50] There were many others before *Filartiga* where the courts were not even concerned about the issue of the defendant's nationality: see, eg, *Adra v Clift*, 195 F Supp 857 (1961).

[51] This is guaranteed by US Const, Art III, s 2, cl 1 and recognised by statute in 28 USC § 1332.

[52] 218 USC § 1350: 'The district courts shall have original jurisdiction of any civil action by an alien for a tort only, committed in violation of the law of nations or a treaty of the United States.'

of recovery not available to Americans. If it does, there might be a serious and totally unexpected issue of unfair discrimination under the equal protection clause of the Fourteenth Amendment recognised and applied under the Fifth Amendment guaranteeing due process in federal cases.[53]

(2) 'In tort only'. The cases and literature have not resolved the meaning of 'tort' at the time the statute was adopted. One author claims that the phrase was used to exclude contract claims deriving from the war of recent memory.[54] But in 1789 the notion of tort was still in its conceptual nascence. Blackstone has no theory of the concept (he mentioned the word but a few times)[55] and therefore it is dubious to read the statute as excluding any particular branch of private law. On the affirmative side, we should say at least that any causes of action founded in trespass and trespass on the case should have been included. The problem is what it was about these actions on these writs that would entail a violation of the law of nations.

We have to think about this problem as it evolved in various stages of history. Since the *Filartiga* decision in 1980 the kinds of torts that qualify as violations of the law of nations are widely condemned, egregious acts of wrongdoing that permit us to think of the ATCA as an instrument of correcting evil. Torture, war crimes, crimes against humanity, genocide—these are the easy cases. But are these the only cases to which the statute could possibly apply?

An instructive example of an older variety of intersection of torts and international law arose in the 1961 case of *Adra v Clift*.[56] The male plaintiff, a Lebanese, and the female defendant, born in Turkey and living in the United States, were married, had a child named Najwa in Beirut, then divorced and began disputing custody of Najwa. The plaintiff argued that under Islamic law applicable in Lebanon, he was entitled to custody after the child reached the

---

[53] US Const Amend V.

[54] William S Dodge, 'The Historical Origins of the Alien Tort Statute: A Response to the Originalists', (1996)19 *Hastings Int'l and Comp L Rev* 222.

[55] The index to vol 3 of the *Commentaries on the Laws of England* concerning private wrongs lists only two references to the word, neither of which is indicative of a general discussion. This is odd in view of Blackstone's very sophisticated opinion about trespass and trespass on the case in *Scott v Shepherd*, 2 *Blackstone's Reports* 892, 96 *Eng Rep* 525 (1773). See the discussion of the case in the text above at n 50.

[56] 195 F Supp 857 (1961).

age of nine. The defendant refused to comply and travelled from country to country (Iraq, France, back to Iraq) in response to offers of employment and in an alleged effort to maintain sole custody of Najwa. In an ATCA action filed in New York, the plaintiff sought a decree for custody, and the defendant sought monetary damages for the failure to pay child support. The interesting question is whether the facts of the case satisfied the requirements both of tort and of a violation of international law.

Until Najwa turned nine, she remained a Lebanese national and therefore was subject to the Lebanese ruling that at the age of nine her father could claim custody under Islamic law. When it came time for the father to claims his rights under this ruling, the mother had Najwa included in her Iraqi passport. The district court identified this unilateral change in her status as a violation of international law.[57] Using the Iraqi passport. the defendant brought her daughter to the United States, thus exposing herself to a suit under the ATCA.

On the question of whether the defendant's actions satisfied the ATCA tort requirement, the court reasoned that the unlawful taking of a child from the custody of its parents is a tort. The court cited as authority the influential treatise by William Prosser,[58] and the Restatement of Torts section 700. The court went on to interpret the father's demand for custody as requested relief in equity and concluded that this would be appropriate in a tort case—citing a long list of authorities.

This is a useful case for exploring the way the element of 'tort' interacts with the element of international law now to be considered.

(3) 'In violation of the Law of Nations or a Treaty of the United States'. This third element in the ATCA relates in various possible ways to the second element, *'in tort only'*. The two could state distinct requirements, they could overlap, or they could inform each other in some other way. Consider again the case of *Adra v Clift*. With the tort established, the court in *Adra v Clift* confronted the question as to whether the tort was committed in violation of international law. On this point the court fell back on the defendant's

---

[57]   *Ibid* at 861. I am not sure what the violation was, perhaps fraud in the receipt of a passport.

[58]   William Prosser 93-93 (2nd edn xxix).

actions with regard to the acquisition of the passport and use of it to enter the United States with Najwa.

Assuming that this point is correct, the court made an inference with far-reaching consequences:

> The wrongful acts were therefore committed in violation of the law of nations. And since they caused direct and special injury to the plaintiff, he may bring an action in tort therefor.[59]

In the *Adra* case the plaintiff lost, despite the sound arguments on his side. In the end the court applied something like the 'best interests of the child' doctrine and ruled that in the light of her age and experience, Najwa should stay with her mother. The case has had little influence as an ATCA precedent. Nonetheless it is important to us because of the various forms of reasoning at work in the argument.

Adra v Clift illustrates two different ways to approach the connection between the requirement of a tort and a violation of the law of nations The first is to establish the tort (unlawful custody) and then show how the same conduct violates the law of nations. In the *Adra* case, however, the logical connection between the two is not very tight. The defendant's tortious behaviour of withholding custody led causally—but not conceptually—to the passport violations. The violations were not logically necessitated by the tortious behaviour. If one person defamed another and the latter tried so hard to flee the jurisdiction that he forged a passport, it would not very sensible to apply the ATCA.

The alternative logic suggested by the court is to posit the international violation first and then to infer injury by making it more difficult for the plaintiff to locate Najwa and to enforce his rights under Lebanese law. That 'direct and special damage' is arguably sufficient to speak of recovery in tort.

Thus we are left with at least two basic strategies: to reason from the nature of tort law to the international violation or, conversely, to reason backwards from the international violation to the damages and remedy that can properly be called tort law.

Two features of the situation support the latter approach. First, as Judge Bork argued in the *Tel-Omer* decision by the DC Circuit,

---

[59] 195 F Supp at 865.

international law never provides a remedy that is self-enforcing in domestic courts.[60] Some national norm is necessary to provide the linkage between the international order and a civil action in a US court. The ATCA uses the term 'tort' broadly to permit the transition from one legal order to another. Thus the language in *Adra* is useful to capture the broad notion of tort as a mode of private relief. William Casto, whose article has had enormous influence in the field,[61] notes that the ATCA does not contain the jurisdictional minimum of 500 dollars found in other other constitutional categories of jurisdiction based on diversity of citizenship. This suggests that 'torts is not understood to refer to a field of law but to a general mode of thinking about liability.

Further, and even more importantly, the notion of tort as it is cultivated in treatises and first-year law courses today barely existed at the time; therefore it makes sense to take the word to refer to wrongs that can be litigated in a court of law. The latest opinion of the Supreme Court—*Sosa v Alvarez-Machain*—stresses the characteristics of the international norms that can be applied in these suits 'in tort only'. They have to be 'specific, universal, and obligatory'.[62] We shall later look more deeply into the origins and meaning of the phrase. The important point is that the Supreme Court uses the expression 'specific, universal, and obligatory' as a watchdog against an overly expansive reading of the ATCA, the terms are characteristics of international norms, not of the law of torts per se.

In short, we should expect either that the concept of tort complements and refines the principle of violating the law of nations or that the law of nations expands our conception of the wrongs that constitute torts.

The ultimate problem is how international law should be made applicable and enforceable in specific cases of tort recovery brought by aliens. The problem bears some resemblance to the long process of incorporation of the Bill of Rights into the due process clause of the Fourteenth Amendment. One by one, most of the first ten

---

[60] *Tel-Oren v Libyan Arab Republic et al*, 726 F 2d 774, DC Circuit (1984) at 798.

[61] See Casto, above n 21.

[62] *Sosa* at 732 (citing *In re Estate of Marcos Human Rights Litigation*, 25 F3d 1467 at 1475 (CA9, 1994) ('Actionable violations of international law must be of a norm that is specific, universal, and obligatory').

amendments were incorporated or 'uploaded' into the due process clause and thus made applicable to the states as a matter of tort law. Now we encounter the reverse process of downloading international law into the ATCA as applied in the federal courts.

In order to engage in this process of downloading, we need to know more about the law of torts as it has evolved since the time of Blackstone. We need to keep two specific practical questions in mind. Does the law of nations as applied under the ATCA incorporate the procedural institutions that drive the law of torts in the United States, namely the jury system, the contingency fee, and punitive damages? Is the latter system of 'incentives' inherent in tort law or does it constitute part of the forum that may be applied regardless of the law of nations? Second, does liability for violating the law of nations include the liability of corporations which are complicit in the violation by supplying the instruments of the violation or providing advice or other facilitating services? Or is the liability of corporations as accessories a matter of tort law to be examined and understood independently of international law? These are difficult questions, which we will not resolve until the end of this book.

5. A PREVIEW OF THE ARGUMENT

Tort law, as it is practised in the United States with the three 'incentive' factors (jury, contingency fees, punitive damages), has become one of the major pillars of western systems of private law. It stands alongside contracts and unjust enrichment as one of three primary institutions in the law of obligations. In addition, in the last 30 years, the field has spawned an enormous body of theory about when and where individuals should have to pay others for the extra-contractual harm they cause. Thus we begin by surveying the law of torts in European and US law, and then we turn to theoretical perspectives that affect the terrain into which the international norms must be planted in order to create a basis for recovery under the ATCA.

The thesis that will emerge, however, is that tort and criminal law intersect in certain cases recognised at the time of Blackstone and interpreted today as falling under the ambit of international criminal law. Thus we will find that international criminal law serves as a very important guide to the proper interpretation of the ATCA. This confirms our underlying intuitions that the ATCA is the American way of seeking universal jurisdiction over the acts that many countries prefer to punish as crimes subject to universal criminal jurisdiction. For a quick summary of the arguments that will be made in this book, you might wish to skip ahead to chapter eight. In the meantime, there is much to learn about the contours of tort law in the twenty-first century.

1

A Comparative Analysis
of Tort Law

The word 'tort' means 'wrong' in French. But the French do not use the word 'tort' to refer to torts. They call it *responsibilité civil* or civil responsibility. The term in English at least communicates some information, namely that torts are wrongs. They represent wrongful action, wrongdoing, violations of rights. The French phrase tells us that if you commit a wrong you will be held civilly responsible. But there are many reasons for civil responsibility—contractual breaches, tort violations, and receiving benefits without justification.

There is a much deeper story behind this difference in terminology. Tort law is associated with the word 'wrong' in the common law because it began its history in close association with criminal wrongdoing. As Blackstone wrote in the mid-eighteenth century, he divided the world of wrongs into public and private wrongs. Public wrongs entail criminal punishment; private wrongs result in liability to pay damages.

In the early common law history of tort law, recovery was based on the writ system, that is, the plaintiff sued on the basis of a writ with a fixed formula issued by the Chancellor of the Exchequer. The law crystallised around the permissibility of using one of this determinate number of writs. The leading writs for the field we now call 'torts' were trespass and trespass on the case. The preoccupation with these particular writs may explain why the concept of tort law was so late in crystallising as a distinct body of law.[1]

---

[1] See the discussion of this and the legacy of the writ system in George P Fletcher and Steve Sheppard, *American Law in a Global Context: The Basics* (New York: Oxford University Press, 2005) [hereinafter referred to as *The Basics*] at 20–21 and 506–9.

Overlapping with criminal law and its principles, the writ of trespass was based essentially on aggression against persons, against land, or against chattels. Trespass against the person was called trespass *vi et armis*, by 'force and arms'. If the trespass was against interests in land it was called trespass *quare clausum fregit*—or intervening in a closed-off space. If against chattels, mere occupation of the goods of another—say by sitting on them—was not enough. The defendant had to pick up and carry off the goods. This was called trespass *de bonis asportatis*.

The first and third of these forms of trespass generated the crimes of assault and battery, on the one hand, and larceny, on the other. Battery is essentially aggression against the person, and larceny consists of acquiring the possession of goods from another and carrying off the same goods. Trespass to land had a different historical function. Because the writ yielded liability simply by entering the land of another, whether knowledgeably or by mistake, it did not generate a felony of unlawful entry (burglary has different roots, probably derivative of the biblical passage, which permits the shooting of a thief 'breaking and entering'[2]). In cases of non-permitted entry to land, because there were no excuses based on ignorance, the writ of trespass provided the best way of testing the plaintiff's claim of the right to possess the land: the plaintiff could recover if and only if he possessed the land and the defendant entered in some way on to the land.[3]

Trespasses against the person and against chattels made more complicated demands on the plaintiff. We shall concentrate here on the defendant's coming into undesired contact with the person of the plaintiff. As we noted, with regard to land, the undesired entry would be enough for liability but bodily friction between persons happens all the time. People brush against each other in the street. They gently put a hand on another's shoulder in order to express support or to suggest that the other move out of the way. They kiss each other on the cheek without asking. In some of these cases the contact is harmful, as in cases of horses or chariots and later cars that get out of control. In order to establish a wrong, something more than the undesirability of the contact is required, but what is that additional element?

---

[2] Exodus 22:2.
[3] See *The Thorns Case*, King's Bench YB 6 Ed 4, f 7, pl 18 (1466).

Today lawyers might say: the injury has to be intentional. But the use of the concept of 'intention' was a late development in the common law. The earlier way of conceptualising tortious trespass was to invoke a concept like directness or immediacy. The paradigm is a punch in the nose.[4] The anti-paradigm—or the case that was not enough for trespass—was something like leaving a roof unfenced or a hole unguarded. The plaintiff walks off the roof or falls into the hole. Whatever directness or immediacy might mean, these elements seem to be absent when the injury occurs as a result of the defendant's creating a dangerous situation and the plaintiff's voluntarily walking into it.

These distinctions date back at least to the Bible. When the defendant directly caused a death—as by using an axe to chop down a tree and the axe blade slips out and hits a bystander—the defendant was not guilty of murder but he had nonetheless to flee to a city of refuge as a sign of his accountability.[5] If the plaintiff fell off an unfenced roof, there were other questions that the court had to ask. How long was the roof unfenced? Did the defendant know about the condition?[6] These are questions that are directed at the factor that today we call the 'fault' of the defendant in allowing the injury to occur.

In the common law, the classic divide was between trespass and a new writ designed to pick up the cases of indirect injury that fell outside the writ of trespass. The new writ was called 'trespass on the case'. We shall call it 'Case' for short.

With the two causes of action overlapping in many borderline cases, it became difficult for lawyers to pick the right writ. If the plaintiff's lawyer picked the wrong writ the defendant could object on procedural grounds and have the case dismissed, sometimes with prejudice. The plaintiff's lawyer's job was to make sure he framed the case on the right writ. This sounds something like jurisdiction today. The first question is always whether you are in the right court or whether you have sued on the right writ. The problem is illustrated by the following classic case decided in 1773.

---

[4] See Richard A Epstein, 'A Theory of Strict Liability' (1973) 2 *Journal of Legal Studies* 151.

[5] Deuteronomy 19:5.

[6] The Bible required builders of new homes to add a 'parapet around your roof so that you may not bring the guilt of bloodshed on your house if someone falls from the roof: Deuteronomy 22:8.

1. THE ORIGINAL 'TICKING BOMB' CASE[7]

The defendant Shepherd threw a lit bomb (called a squib) into a crowded marketplace. It landed near Yates. A bystander named Willis intervened to save himself and Yates. He threw the bomb further within the marketplace, Then Ryal picked it up and for the same fear of harm threw it across the market where it finally exploded and put out Scott's eye. This would have been a simple case if Scott had sued Ryal in trespass. Whether Ryal acted under pressure or not, Ryal threw a ticking bomb at Scott and injured him severely. Perhaps if he had not thrown the bomb, perhaps if it had just bounced off his stand, there might have been an argument that it was not Ryal's doing at all. An implicit requirement of trespass *vi et armis* is that the action injuring another must be at least the action of another human being. The agent must be connected to the injury, and the minimal connection is expressed in the idea that his action causes the harm.[8]

Another way to put this minimal requirement—a terminology more used in Continental Europe than in the United States—is that the harm must be *attributable* to the defendant as an agent. Attribution means to hold to account, laying to the charge of the defendant. If the bomb just bounced off the back of his head, it would not be chargeable to his agency. The minimal requirement of trespass can be restated as: the harm must be directly attributable to the action of the defendant.

The general theory of attribution includes three dimensions, all three of them relevant to *Scott v Shepherd*. The first question, already noted, is whether the harm-causing events derives from the action of the defendant. The second question is of causation. If Shepherd did not cause the harm he is not liable—under any theory of tort liability. The third factor, also subtly raised in this case, is that if the action of the defendant was excused by coercion or mistake, the harm would not be attributable to him. In short, any of the following three claims can stop the argument for liability dead

---

[7] *Scott v Shepherd*, 2 *Blackstone's Reports* 892, 96 Eng Rep 525 (1773). The case is reproduced in Fletcher and Sheppard, *American Law in a Global Context: The Basics* (pub details, 2005) 28 [page cites are to *The Basics*].

[8] This requirement is elaborately developed today in the theory of criminal law. See *The Grammar*, (2007), ch 6.

in its tracks: (1) no relevant action on the part of the defendant; (2) no relevant causal connection to the harm; or (3) a valid excuse for causing harm.

These problems are complicated in *Scott v Shepherd* because of the triple-play feature: Shepherd to Yates; Willis to Ryal; Ryal to Scott. The intervening acts become a source of perplexity. Are they relevant to the problems of action, causation, or excuse?

As was common at the time, the jury decided that Scott deserved compensation of 100 pounds but reserved the question of liability for judges to decide on the facts established. The case then went up to the King's Bench to solicit the opinion of five judges, recorded for us to study in the English Reports. The issue, we should remind ourselves, was whether it was correct for Scott to sue Shepherd on a writ of trespass. If the court decided against, he still might have an action for recovery in Case.

The famous judge on the panel was William Blackstone, who had just published his monumental four-volume work *Commentaries on the Laws of England* in the years 1765 to 1769. Now a few years later he writes an opinion about trespass and Case that is more sophisticated than what he has to say about private wrongs in his *Commentaries*.

Blackstone starts off his opinion boldly by claiming that the action of trespass will not lie. He took the settled distinction to be whether the injury is direct and immediate, on the one hand, or mediate and consequential, on the other. If the former, then trespass would lie; if the latter, the remedy was in Case.[9] This is a variation on the theme of causation. A direct causal link is one that runs straight from the defendant to the plaintiff. An indirect connection goes round about and appears to tie the defendant less closely to the injury.

Blackstone then dismisses the criterion proposed by his colleague Nares that the critical question was whether the throwing of the bomb was lawful.[10] This is a plausible position but, for reasons I will explain later, Blackstone will have none of it. He announces that he will explain why the injury was indirect or consequential and therefore not subject to liability in trespass.

---

[9] His cite for this proposition is *Reynolds and Clarke, Lord Raym* 1401, Stra 634 (*The Basics* at 29).

[10] *The Basics* at 29.

In the following lines he introduces a few critical concepts that facilitate his argument. He describes Willis and Ryal as 'free agents'. They have a right to protect themselves by throwing the bomb to another place. They both acted on their own 'judgement'. There was 'new motion' impressed on the squib. All these words are designed, rhetorically, to undermine the causal attribution of the injury to Shepherd.

Imagine a different set of words to describe the same transaction. Willis and Ryal are not free; they are compelled to act. They responded instinctively to save their own lives. They acted not on judgement but out of fear and panic. They were simply 'boosters' in the original motion imparted to the bomb when Shepherd threw it.

Lawyers learn very quickly that there is no correct way to describe a set of facts. If Blackstone chose the former set of terms, he prepared the way for a conclusion that the harm was consequential. If a lawyer chose the latter set of terms he would take a long step towards proving that the injury was direct and that Shepherd was liable under trespass.

Blackstone goes further in his opinion and sets up a matrix for which every judge and lawyer should be thankful. His choice of language makes the case different 'from the cases put (apparently in argument) of turning loose a wild beast or a madman'. In the latter cases, as you can easily see, the language of 'free agents' and 'judgement' and 'rights' would not apply to the wild beast or the madman. These are cases where trespass would clearly lie. But a paradigm case like that of the wild beast is not useful unless the judge or advocate also provides the contrary case that stands obviously for the application of Case. Blackstone gives an example to stake out the territory of Case:

> If a man tosses a football into the street, and, after being kicked about by one hundred people, it at last breaks a tradesman's window, shall he have trespass against the man who first produced it?

This is a wonderful counter-example, a *reductio ad absurdam* of imposing liability for trespass against Shepherd. But there seem to be many grounds for claiming that the ticking bomb case differs radically from that of the football. First, there is no need to kick the ball further and, so far as there is a danger necessitating throwing the bomb further, Shepherd is responsible for that danger.

Be that as it may, it is important to recognise there is no right answer in this battle of the analogies. It would be like asking whether a circle is more like a triangle or like an oblong. For certain purposes, a circle is like both, compact and symmetrical like a triangle, curved like an oblong. Without a theory specifying which perspective matters and why, there is no way of deciding whether a circle is more like one figure or another. The same is true with the facts in *Scott v Shepherd*. There is no way, in principle, to decide whether the facts are more like the defendant's releasing a wild beast into the streets or the defendant's plus a hundred others' kicking a football around. Blackstone decided this case was more like kicking the football around than releasing a wild beast that causes damages. His conclusion is by no means the only plausible choice.

The general point is that the logical relationship 'X is more like Y than like Z' is not a proposition that can be said to be true or false. It is not a logical deduction. Perhaps there are some clear cases: New York is more like Paris than it is like New Haven; but even there some people might disagree.

There is an important truth to be learned here about legal reasoning. Like all judges and lawyers, Blackstone would like to pretend that the decision is based on a rule, namely the rule that trespass requires a direct and immediate injury. The problem is that in practice the rules—particularly the rules of tort law—are too vague to dictate clear results. In the end the process of decision requires an analogical matrix of the form: Is this case more like Y (where we agree the answer is one way) than it is like Z (where we agree the answer is the other way)? Blackstone's opinion in *Scott v Shepherd* brilliantly lays out this mode of thinking, which is present whether we like it or not in virtually all cases of tort law.

Blackstone's opinion deserves to be remembered but it did not carry the day. There were five judges on the King's Bench. Blackstone was the only one to decide that trespass did not lie, that perhaps the defendant was liable but the plaintiff would have to sue in Case. Three judges agreed with Blackstone's formulation of the law, at least with regard to the rule that trespass requires a 'direct and immediate injury'. They do not restate his analogical matrix, rather they introduce numerous phrases that emphasise the connections between trespass and criminal law. In Chief Justice de Grey's opinion, trespass is not simply trespass as it is for Blackstone, it is *vi et armis*, with 'force and violence'.[11] The defendant's action was

---

[11] *Ibid* at 32.

'unlawful' (a factor not mentioned by Blackstone). When harmful consequences follow from an unlawful action, the argument goes, the defendant is responsible: 'Every one who does an unlawful act is considered as the doer of all that follows.'[12] This is not a sound principle of criminal law because it ignores the factor of personal culpability for the specific deed, but it is nonetheless expressed in rules like the felony–murder and misdemeanour–manslaughter rules of criminal liability. You break the law and you pay for the consequences. The fifth judge also took this line: throwing a lit bomb was unlawful and therefore the defendant had to pay for the resulting damage. The emphasis is on the danger to the public as a whole—indeed, a proper concern of the criminal law. But this is not the language of private law as it is developed by Blackstone. And it is not an analysis of the procedural differences between trespass and Case. The reasoning of the majority is quite simple: if you endanger the public by breaking the law, you pay for the consequences.

This is not a tenable principle—neither of tort law nor of criminal law. Today we would label the problem 'proximate cause'. It cannot be the law that the thrower of a bomb is liable for all possible consequences. Suppose the bomb landed on the ground and before Ryal could throw it further, Willis—not seeing it—tripped over it and breaks his leg. Is Shepherd liable for the broken leg? Why should he be? First this is a question obviously of Case, not of trespass, and the problem with imposing liability on Shepherd is that the injury appears to be Willis's fault. He should have looked where he was going.

By posing his example of the hundred people who kick around a football, Blackstone was raising a slightly different problem in the field of 'proximate cause'. If someone kicks a football through the window of a tradesman, he is liable in trespass to land. No questions asked. But if 99 other people kick the ball before it goes through the window, there is a problem not only of directness but whether the original kicker caused the damage at all. The 99 others are called 'intervening causes'. Each starts the causal chain all over again. Proximate cause is one of the thorniest problems in the entire law of torts. It is of critical importance in most of the

---

[12] *Ibid.*

possible claims that arise under the ATCA. In due course we shall explore the problem in depth and show how it matters in cases of liability for human rights abuses.

What can we learn from the original case of the ticking bomb? In Blackstone's opinion we get a very careful analysis of the difference between trespass and Case, with the conclusion that the plaintiff loses on procedural grounds. The proper writ, says the great jurist, would have been Case rather than trespass. It turns out that none of the other judges was really interested in this procedural nicety. (Does this tell us something about the relationship of academics to practising judges?) In the opinions favouring liability, although with lip service to the theory of trespass and Case, the argument is directed to the element of public danger in throwing a lit bomb into the marketplace.

Blackstone's opinion establishes for us the five essential elements of trespass, which are as follows. First, there must be an action on the part of the defendant. If A throws B off a roof and B lands on C, C can sue A in trespass but not B. B was merely the instrument of the harm. This requirement is typically not discussed. It is assumed as a common element in both criminal and tort liability.

Second, the defendant's action must be the cause in fact of the plaintiff's injury. If the injury would have occurred anyway, the defendant is not liable. This requirement is expressed in the *sine qua non* or 'necessity' test of causation. If it had not been for the defendant's action, the damage would not have occurred. This counterfactual test (you have to imagine the world without the defendant's act and ask whether the damage would have occurred anyway) is difficult to apply and it is open to many theoretical objections as well. Yet work-a-day lawyers use it all the time and therefore we explain the requirement of causation as a relationship of necessity between the cause and effect.

The third requirement is the subtle issue of proximate cause, given short shrift in Blackstone's opinion, but which we assess in some detail in the *Palsgraf* case below. The result might be attributable to the defendant's action under the 'but for' test but it might nonetheless be so far removed from the original causal force that it should be considered an independent force. This would have been the case if Willis had had plenty of time to intervene and nonetheless exercised defensive action after calm reflection. His independent deliberation would have broken the causal chain from Shepherd to Scott. The issue of direct and indirect causation discussed in

Blackstone's opinion approaches this problem but only in the context of classifying the case as one arising in trespass or in Case.

The fourth factor is a restatement of the issue of excuses, as mentioned above. In a pure case of trespass, we suppose that there were originally no excuses allowed. But then a case occurred in which the defendant was firing his musket and just at that moment, the plaintiff ran into the path of the bullet. This was called an 'inevitable accident'[13] and became the official source of excuses under the writ of trespass. Eventually, the issue of excuses became the reciprocal side of the fault of negligence. If there was a valid excuse, there was no fault, and vice versa. In its pure and typical form, as seen in *Scott v Shepherd*, the writ of trespass did not require an analysis of fault. It is important to keep this in mind because the requirement of fault remains one of the most highly controversial issues in all of tort law.

The fifth and final requirement in all tort cases is whether the plaintiff suffered a compensable damage. This is not problematic in *Scott v Shepherd* because the plaintiff lost an eye. If that is not damage, nothing is. But whether fright, insult, embarrassment, shock and other borderline harms qualify as tort 'damage' is one of the issues that has occupied the courts for centuries. In *Adra v Clift*, discussed in the Introduction, the damage was taking a child from the lawful custody of its parent. This illustrates that the elements of damages in tort need not be as concrete as in *Scott v Shepherd*.

To summarise the five elements of trespass, as Blackstone implicitly understood them to be: (1) an action, (2) a cause of harm, (3) an exception for aberrant causation, (4) an exception for excuses, and (5) actual compensable damage.

If these common elements are satisfied, we should inquire, as did Blackstone, about the proper writ—trespass or Case. The choice is not simply a procedural issue. Underlying the choice is a deeper struggle about the nature of tort liability. Blackstone thought of tort law as private law, as a matter of private wrongs, one person against another. The majority of the court associated tort liability more with the principles of public law applicable in criminal cases: the critical element was the unlawful action, the danger to the public, expressed in the throwing of the bomb into the marketplace. The battle for the soul of tort law was just beginning.

---

[13] *Weaver v Ward*, 80 ER 284 (KB, 1616).

2. THE ATTEMPT TO RECONCILE TRESPASS AND CASE

At first blush trespass looks like a form of strict liability, that is, liability without fault, and Case, a cause of action based on fault. There is something to this. The ordinary case of trespass did not require proof of any fault, intention, or culpability on the part of the defendant. Under the writ of Case, for example if Willis trips over the bomb without seeing it, the analysis of liability requires not only attribution of the damage to the defendant's act but an assessment of the fault of both parties. (We leave aside for the moment the early consideration of 'inevitable accident' as a preliminary form of fault in trespass.)

In the nineteenth century the writs of the common law came into disrepute. They were eventually abolished in the 1870s.[14] Even before their formal rejection, the mood of the courts was to find ways to unify the elements of tort liability. This mood is exemplified in a case that came to the Supreme Court of Massachusetts in 1850. The subtle factual pattern and the sophisticated legal analysis in *Brown v Kendall*[15] make it the leading exemplar of the unified theory of tort liability. Kendall used a stick to break up a dog fight between his dog and Brown's. Brown was standing behind him as the defendant moved around to engage the fighting dogs. At one point, Kendall lifted his stick and hit Brown in the eye, resulting in a severe injury. Again, the plaintiff lost an eye. Again, the question: should this be a problem of trespass or of Case?

At least four of the five basic requirements are easily satisfied. The defendant had acted, thereby causing in fact and proximately damage to the plaintiff, and the plaintiff suffered damage. Also the case seems to be a direct injury to the plaintiff. The biggest problem is the possibility of an analogy to the case of the plaintiff who runs into the path of the musket fire. This plaintiff was also moving around. Thus the fourth requirement is in question: could not the defendant invoke an excuse of 'inevitable accident'?

In fact the trial judge instructed the jury to find for the defendant if the defendant could prove 'the exercise of extraordinary care, so that the accident was inevitable, using the word not in a strict but a popular sense'.[16] Notice how by 1850 the principle of 'inevitable

---

[14] See *The Basics* at 26.
[15] 60 *Mass* 292, 6 *Cush* 292 (1850).
[16] *Ibid* at 297.

accident' has expanded from the status of an extreme exception to encompass every case in which the defendant is exercising 'ordinary care'. In other words, if the defendant can prove that there was no fault on his part, no negligence, no want of ordinary care, there was no liability in trespass. Thus, the trial court had come close to merging trespass and Case into one standard of liability based on fault.

But note two debts to the traditional conception of trespass. First, the burden of persuasion was still on the defendant to prove the absence of fault. And second, there was no reference in the instructions to the jury on the relevance of the plaintiff's fault. In fact, traditionally, under both trespass and Case, the negligence of the plaintiff was irrelevant. The first time that the common law courts spoke about the relevance of contributory negligence was in the early nineteenth century.[17] Usually these problems were addressed under the writ of Case by asking simply whether the defendant was at fault when the plaintiff negligently brought on his own injury. Another way to arrive at the same doctrinal result was to say that the defendant was not the cause of the injury when the plaintiff appeared to be the primary cause. Whatever the doctrinal foundations, the carving out of the plaintiff's contribution as a totally distinct question in the analysis of liability was a turning point in the law of torts.

It is one thing to analyse liability on the basis of what the defendant—and just the defendant—did to the victim. This is the way we typically think of criminal cases. The theory of liability comes into different focus when liability hinges on the interaction between the parties. This way of thinking is more in the spirit of private law—analogous to the law of contracts. Conceptualising the plaintiff's fault as a critical factor takes us therefore from torts as an offshoot of criminal law to torts as an independent branch of private law. This is the turning point symbolised by *Brown v Kendall*.

On the instructions as given at trial, the injured plaintiff won. But the High Court of Massachusetts reversed, with a path-breaking judgment by Chief Justice Shaw. The opinion takes the final steps to merge trespass and Case. The first was the minor adjustment of requiring the plaintiff to prove the defendant's negligence or want of

---

[17] The case usually cited is *Butterfield v Forrester*, 103 ER 926 (KB, 1809).

ordinary care (no need for further use of the language of 'inevitable accident'). The more dramatic step was introducing the element of the plaintiff's fault. In the unified theory of tort liability the plaintiff would have to prove the absence of his own fault in order to establish liability. Later we shall consider how this factor of the plaintiff's fault should be conceptualised—as contributory negligence, which implies that the defendant is not liable at all, or as comparative negligence, which serves to reduce the liability of the defendant in proportion to the plaintiff's fault.

Note that both of these changes have the political effect of aiding defendants in their efforts to resist liability. The cases that we have been discussing are individuals suing individuals, but the doctrines these cases formulate have implications for the entire field of liability, notably cases of customers, employees, and other victims suing large corporations. They also have significant implications for individuals suing corporations for aiding and facilitating governments that engage in human rights abuses. Thus disputes about throwing squibs in the public market or breaking up dog fights carry vast, long-range implications.

By the time that Oliver Wendell Holmes, Jr wrote his classic work *The Common Law* in 1881, it appeared that the fault standard, as reflected in *Brown v Kendall* had triumphed and become the guiding standard of tort liability for the future.[18] Unfortunately, neither life nor the law was so simple.

3. THE 'BIRTH' OF STRICT LIABILITY

In the days of trespass and Case, no one ever spoke about strict liability. There was no requirement to prove fault in trespass but that is because 'directly causing injury' was considered a sufficient basis for imposing liability. Some scholars spoke of these cases, as did Holmes, with disdain, as cases of 'acting at one's peril'. Fault— that is, negligence on the part of the defendant and no negligence on the part of the plaintiff—appeared to be the correct normative

---

[18] See Oliver W Holmes, *The Common Law*, ed Mark Dewolfe Howe (Cambridge, MA, Harvard University Press, 1963, originally published 1881) [hereafter cited as *Common Law*].

standard. But no one in the nineteenth century ever explained why fault should be the exclusive standard of liability. More recently, Ernest Weinrib has argued for the principle of fault as the only correct solution to the conflict between respecting the freedom of the defendant to act and the rights of the plaintiff to be secure in his or her person.[19] The fault standard has had an undeniable appeal, but the law of trespass and its coming close to liability without fault was deeply entrenched in the common law. As Maitland said, the forms of actions may be buried but they rule us from the grave.[20] As soon as it appeared that the fault standard was going to dominate the law of torts, however, the alternative of strict liability—or liability without fault—became a more respectable possibility.

In the phrase 'liability without fault,' fault can refer to one of two dimensions of liability. It can refer to whether the activity causing harm is socially permissible and lawful, or it can refer to whether the defendant is personally accountable for taking the risk. For example, the activity of throwing the bomb in *Scott v Shepherd* was not permissible and the defendant was unquestionably accountable and at fault for choosing to throw the bomb. In *Brown v Kendall*, the activity of breaking up the dog fight was in itself permissible and lawful. There was no fault in the activity as such. If there was fault on the defendant's side, it was for the way he executed the activity.

This distinction might not be so obvious, but it is of critical importance. In the theory of criminal law, the distinction is formulated as the cleavage between wrongdoing and culpability—between violating a norm and personal accountability for the violation. The term 'fault' can refer to either dimension of liability. Thus strict liability or liability without fault can refer to either (1) liability without wrongdoing or (2) liability without personal accountability. In criminal cases, it would not be conceptually coherent to impose liability without wrongdoing, that is, punishment for conduct that is socially permissible would not be coherent.[21] But liability without personal accountability for the specific harm (or at least without proof of personal fault) is coherent—perhaps unjust, but coherent.

---

[19] Ernest Weinrib, *The Idea of Private Law* (Harvard University Press, 1995).
[20] Friedrich W Maitland, *Lectures on Equity and the Forms of Action* (Cambridge, Cambridge University Press, 1909) at 296.
[21] This argument is developed in *The Grammar* at 34–7.

In tort cases, however, we should think of strict liability differently. It is liability for engaging in certain kinds of permissible and lawful activities. It would be impossible to impose criminal liability in these cases but tort liability makes sense and might be the right thing to do.

These considerations become relevant in the study of the leading English case of *Rylands v Fletcher*. The dispute started when one Fletcher built a reservoir on land adjacent to the property of Rylands. Unbeknownst to both parties, there were old coalmining tunnels under the land. Rylands started mining for coal on his land. He accidentally broke into the old tunnels and the defendant's reservoir flooded his land. In the Court of Exchequer two judges voted against liability, and the famous Judge Bramwell—known for his efforts to hold industry liable for the consequences of its activities—voted for liability. The plaintiff's first appeal was to the Exchequer Chamber, where the judges formulated the issue that the plaintiff could recover only by showing some 'default' by the defendant. They concluded that the defendant himself was free from fault but the engineers he selected had acted without proper care.

Judge Blackburn of the Exchequer Chamber developed a theory of liability that, as we shall see, resembles the principle accepted a half-century before in the French *Code Civil*. The judges perceived the defendant's building the reservoir as 'bring[ing] on his land something which, though harmless while it remains there, will naturally do mischief if it escape out of his land'. The judges reasoned that the cases of liability for straying animals supported a general principle of liability, regardless of fault, for all foreign substances escaping from one person's land to another's. The expression they used to express the idea of liability without fault is 'acting at one's peril'. Holmes also used this expression in 1881 to describe the alternative to the fault standard, which, in his view, had become the reigning standard in the common law. As I have suggested, however, 'strict liability' is not a case in which the defendant is held liable regardless of personal accountability; rather it is a case in which engaging in the particular activity—lawful as it may be—becomes a proper basis for imposing liability for harmful consequences.

The House of Lords affirmed liability and provided a better foundation for liability without fault. The difficulty with Blackburn's principle can be seen at once. It could not be the case that all escaping mischievous substance would generate liability. What if all the property owners in the region burned fires on their land, but in one case the fire escaped—without fault—and caused harm to the neighbouring property. Or suppose it is an oil-drilling region. All the neighbours have pools of oil, but one drains into the land of another. Oil is the kind of substance that can do damage when it escapes. Is there any reason to impose liability when both sides create and are exposed to the same risk? It seems that when things are kept on one body of land and they wander over to another body of land, something more than displacement of the thing should be required for liability. The analysis of liability in these cases needs more refinement.

In his opinion for the House of Lords, Lord Cairns added a factor that may seem quaint to some, but which in fact explains our intuitions in the case: If the defendant accumulated water or any other substance in the 'natural' use of his land and the substance escaped, he would not be liable to his neighbour in the absence of fault. In this case the Exchequer Chamber had recognised that the engineers who planned and constructed the reservoir might have been at fault but they were apparently sufficiently independent of the defendant that their fault was not imputable to him (in modern terms we would call the engineers 'independent contractors'). Therefore the only basis for finding that the defendant 'acted as his peril' was that the use of the land was non-natural.

The use of the term 'natural' in the House of Lords' opinion has not received much attention or respect in the reception of the case in the common law. It sounds too mystical and too hostile to the idea of change in the social interest. The best way to interpret Cairns' opinion is to think of the natural use of the land as something like the normal or conventional use, something that can change from time to time but which, for any particular region, constitutes the norm of proper behaviour. Under these conditions of normalcy, all the landowners impose risks on the others and therefore none is liable for the damage that can be expected to occur. Interpreted in this way, *Rylands v Fletcher* provides the core example of a general paradigm of liability which, in chapter three, I shall call the paradigm of non-reciprocal risk-taking. When all sides in an activity impose on each other reciprocal risks, then none is liable to the others for the realisation of the risk in concrete damage.

In *Rylands*, the defendant did something out of the ordinary. He built a reservoir in coalmining country and accumulated water in an artificially dug basin. When Lord Cairns described this use of the land as 'non-natural,' he should be read to have meant something like abnormal and unconventional.

In the vast body of law that has emerged from *Rylands v Fletcher*—not only about land but about all activities that impose extraordinary risks on others—the key factor has been the conventional or 'normal' nature of the activity. The basic principle of strict liability is now recognised in the Restatement (Second) of Torts §520, labelled 'Abnormally Dangerous Activities'. According to the drafters, six factors enter into the analysis whether an activity is abnormally dangerous and therefore a proper subject of liability without fault. Of course, it is of some importance whether there is 'high degree of risk'. Low-risk activities are not likely to generate strict liability under any circumstances, but there are many high-risk activities—driving cars, carrying rifles, flying aeroplanes, for example. These activities rarely result in liability without fault.

Whether building a reservoir in *Rylands* was a low-risk activity depends a great deal on the description of the case. If you only know what a reasonable person might have known about the shaft below, then it was a low-risk activity. If you had special knowledge of the shafts below, then of course—from your perspective—it was high risk. This is a general problem in the theory of risk. There are no high and low risks in the abstract. It all depends on how much you know about the circumstances leading to the accident.

The key factors shaping strict liability, I submit, are to be found not in attempts to quantify the risk as high or low, but by focusing on that quaint concept in the House of Lords' opinion: 'the non-natural use of land'. Two of six factors mentioned in the Restatement are readily interpreted as modern interpretations of what it means to engage in 'natural' activities. The natural should be understood as the conventional and the appropriate, as suggested by this wording of the Restatement:

> §520. In determining whether an activity is abnormally dangerous, the following factors are to be considered:
>
> ...;
> (d) [the] extent to which the activity is not a matter of common usage;
> (e) [the] inappropriateness of the activity to the place where it is carried on.

Thus, if the activity is common and appropriate to its place, it is natural and therefore not an apt basis for strict liability. In their commentaries, the drafters connect their general standard to the language of *Rylands v Fletcher*:

> Water collected in large quantity in a hillside reservoir in the midst of a city or in coal mining country is not the activity of any considerable portion of the population, and may therefore be regarded as abnormally dangerous.

In other cases, for example, the collection of bodies of water—in pipes or cisterns—is not abnormal, and therefore the principle of strict liability does not apply. It would have been helpful for the judges to give illustrations of the polar paradigms, as Blackstone did in *Scott v Shepherd*. A 'natural' animal would presumably be one that was common in the neighbourhood, for example household pets in the suburbs, and a non-natural animal would be one likely to be found in a zoo, for example lions or tigers. For all their sound intuitions, however, the drafters fail to set up the necessary contrast between the cases that are clearly within the rule and those clearly outside the rule.

Instead, they provide criteria for a deductive application of the rule but they never explain why their six criteria justify strict liability. And, in fact, one of their six is clearly false. Point six refers to the '[the] extent to which its value to the community is outweighed by its dangerous attributes'. The important feature of strict liability is that if the activity is valuable to the community, then it cannot be prohibited. For example, a cement company may pollute the air and make life in the vicinity of the plant unhealthy, but the courts will not enjoin a valuable industry from operating. Because an injunction is impossible, there is an even stronger case for imposing a duty to compensate those injured.[22]

Cost–benefit analysis has its place in other aspects of tort law but not in the theory of strict liability. The problem with the Restatement's pot-pourri is that it has variables but it offers neither clear paradigms nor a theory of liability. For that matter, the court in *Rylands* never explained why it should matter whether the use of land is natural or not. As I shall explain in greater detail in the next chapter, the principle of strict liability as it evolved from *Rylands* to

---

[22] *Boomer v Atlantic Cement Co*, 26 NY2d 219, 257 NE2d 870, 309 NYS2d 312 (1970).

the second Restatement exemplifies a paradigm of liability, which I dubbed some time ago and which has since been recognised in the literature as the 'paradigm of reciprocity'.[23] A paradigm of liability is more than doctrine, more than a set of intuitively plausible criteria. It is a theory of liability, a principle grounded in moral and political thought justifying the imposition of liability for causing harm.

4. PROXIMATE CAUSE: THE LAST GASP OF TRESPASS

The merger of trespass and Case in the nineteenth century did not prevent the courts from relying further on the concept of direct injury. Although the concept no longer defined a cause of action, as Blackstone thought it did in the eighteenth century, it entered often into the analysis of proximate cause, that is, defining the extent of liability once it was established that the defendant negligently caused the injury to the plaintiff. In a case that was the favourite of the late Professor Harry Kalven, Jr, the leading theorist of tort law in his time, a schoolchild kicked a playmate in the tibia after the teacher called the class to order.[24] Unbeknownst to the defendant, the plaintiff had a very sensitive wound on his leg exactly at the spot where he was kicked. The playful kick resulted in serious injuries—the gravity of which was totally unexpected. The court analysed liability by applying a doctrinal formula that had its origins in *Brown v Kendall*: 'either the defendant must be at fault or the intention must be unlawful'.[25] As to the scope of the injuries, the defendant was clearly not at fault. But the kick could be interpreted as an intentional assault and battery. Was the intention unlawful? The court reasoned that if the victim did not consent, and the defendant knew this to be true, his intention was unlawful. But that would make him liable only for grazing the leg. Is he also liable for the unexpected consequences? As to this question—the extent of liability for battery—the court applied the basic principle of trespass. The harm was the direct consequence

[23] George P Fletcher, 'Fairness and Utility in Tort Theory' (1972) 85 *Harvard Law Review* 537.
[24] *Vosburg v Putney*, 78 Wis 84 (1890).
[25] *Brown v Kendall*, 60 Mass 292 (1850).

of the kick and therefore the defendant was liable for the full scope of the injuries.

This makes some sense, but only if we understand and appreciate the ingrained influence of the writ of trespass. In the kick case, at least we can say that the kick establishes threshold liability for battery, and factors of directness enter only at the second stage of analysis, when we seek to establish the scope of liability. But the factor of 'directness' has also played a strong role in the threshold question of liability for unexpected damages. In the famous *Polemis* case,[26] decided in 1921 by the King's Bench, the defendant seaman had inadvertently kicked a plank into the hold of a ship. The plank's hitting bottom triggered a spark, which set off an explosion. The court affirmed liability on the basis of negligence in kicking the board. The explosion was the direct consequence of the negligent act.

There is some controversy about whether *Polemis* follows the same analysis as *Vosburg*, the schoolboy kick case. Is the factor of directness about the threshold of liability for negligence or is it about the scope of damages? Calling it 'proximate cause' does not necessarily solve this question. The problem lies in the theory of negligence. Is a negligent act a wrong, just like the schoolboy kick? In that case, at least, we could identify the victim before inquiring about the scope of liability. In *Polemis* the danger is to society in the abstract. Thus we come face to face again with the problem debated between Blackstone and the majority in *Scott v Shepherd*. Is the wrong committed in a tort case a wrong against a specific individual, the plaintiff, or is it a wrong against society?

In the much-taught *Palsgraf* case, decided in New York in 1928, this question was debated with a level of sophistication rarely encountered in the opinions of judges (or in the law reviews, for that matter). The factual pattern is by now familiar. As Chief Justice Cardozo eloquently reports:

> Plaintiff was standing on a platform of defendant's railroad after buying a ticket to go to Rockaway Beach. A train stopped at the station, bound for another place. Two men ran forward to catch it. One of the men reached the platform of the car without mishap, though the train was already moving. The other man, carrying a package, jumped aboard the

---

[26] *In re Polemis* [1921] 3 KB 560.

car, but seemed unsteady as if about to fall. A guard on the car, who had held the door open, reached forward to help him in, and another guard on the platform pushed him from behind. In this act, the package was dislodged, and fell upon the rails. It was a package of small size, about fifteen inches long, and was covered by a newspaper. In fact it contained fireworks, but there was nothing in its appearance to give notice of its contents. The fireworks when they fell exploded. The shock of the explosion threw down some scales at the other end of the platform, many feet away. The scales struck the plaintiff, causing injuries for which she sues.[27]

Note the abstractness of the description. No one is mentioned by name. This way of thinking about tort law—in the abstract—disturbed Judge John Noonan so much that he wrote a book about it.[28] Interestingly, however, Cardozo CJ notes that Ms Palsgraf had bought a ticket to go to Rockaway Beach. This factor potentially brought the case within the law of contract but, as is the practice in the common law, these cases at the borderline of contract and tort are treated as torts. One reason for this preference is that the damages are more generous in torts cases: they include pain and suffering. As we shall see below, German law traditionally had reasons for preferring to treat these cases as problems of contract rather than tort.[29] The distinction between tort and contract is, of course, of utmost relevance for the ATCA because the federal statute recognises liability *in tort only* for violations of the law of nations.

There was no problem in *Palsgraf* as to whether the actions of the two guards were imputable to the Long Island Railroad Company. They were employees and—in contrast to the independent contractors in *Rylands v Fletcher*—the principle of *respondeat superior* charges all torts committed by agents to their employers. This is true at least with respect to all torts committed on the job in technical language 'within the scope of employment'.

The plaintiff Ms Palsgraf recovered damages in a jury, and the judgment was affirmed on appeal to the appellate division. You

[27] *Palsgraf v Long Island RR* 248 NY 339 (1928).
[28] John T Noonan, Jr, *Persons and Masks of the Law* (New York, Farrar, Straus & Giroux, 1976).
[29] This preference was based on the stricter rule of *respondeat superior* in contract cases. Compare BGB §831 (employer excused if not at fault) with BGB §228 (*respondeat superior* applied in contract cases).

would expect the plaintiff to have won in the Court of Appeals, the highest appellate court of New York. But Cardozo CJ's abstract beginning might be considered a sign that the court was less than sympathetic to these victims. An opinion for the plaintiff would have emphasised at the outset the gravity of the injuries and the importance of deferring an appeal to the wisdom of the jury in imposing liability. Cardozo never mentions the injury to Ms. Palsgraf or to her children.

From these signs we might well expect an opinion to uphold the side of railroad, although on the facts it is a little difficult to imagine. After all, the Railroad Company's agents were negligent; someone who bought a ticket suffered injury. This seems like a clear case for recovery.

Cardozo CJ had no particular sympathy for the railroad,[30] but there was one legal issue he wanted to get right. He had the same concern for conceptual purity that motivated Blackstone in *Scott v Shepherd*. As the choice of proper writ took precedence for one judge, the right formulation of the legal duty to Ms Palsgraf preoccupied CJ Cardozo.

Duty? We have not mentioned this issue in our survey of relevant tort issues to this point. Indeed, in the heartland of tort law, duty is irrelevant. Or to put it more precisely, the duty not to cause injury by aggressive action is simply assumed. The only place where there is an issue about duty is in the analysis of liability for omissions. The universal rule is that there is no liability unless the person omitting to rescue has a violated a duty to aid the party in distress. These duties generally arise in relationships, and therefore we can generalise: liability for aggressive injuries does not depend on quality of the relationship with the victim, but liability for omission presupposes a relationship that gives rise to a duty of care.

Liability for negligence is generally considered a failure to exercise a duty of case. The conceptual framework, therefore, is of omissions. Those who summarise the law in black-letter rules tend to identify duty as a fundamental requirement of negligence.[31] They think in the conceptual framework of Case. In trespass, duty

---

[30] In *Hynes v New York C R Co*, 231 N.Y. 229 (1921), Cardozo CJ found for an adolescent plaintiff who was trespassing on a railroad bridge, using a spur from it to dive into the river.

[31] Some scholars have taken the element seriously. see John CP Goldberg and Benjamin C Zipursky, *The Restatement (Third) and the Place of Duty in Negligence Law*, 54 *Vanderbilt Law Review* 657 (2001).

was never an issue. When A affirmatively strikes B, as in *Scott v Shepherd* or *Brown v Kendall*, it is assumed that everyone is under a duty not to injury others by direct or intentional action.

For Judge Andrews, the dissenting judge in *Palsgraf*, the issue of duty was secondary. The primary question was negligence as an unlawful act against the public (recall the views opposed to Blackstone in *Scott v Shepherd*). He thought of negligent conduct as a form of aggression against the possible victims akin to A striking B in the trespass cases. Why then did the issue loom so large for Judge Cardozo? Did he think of negligence as an omission a failure for which the defendant would be liable only on the basis of a special relationship with the victim?

One explanation is that at the time Cardozo had 'duty' on the mind. He had just a resolved a major dispute in the field of product liability by redefining the duty of manufacturers to consumers. The issue in *MacPherson v Buick*[32] was whether the consumer—injured when the wheel of his Buick collapsed—could sue the manufacturer for a defect in a car purchased from a retailer. The consumer who bought from a retailer had no direct contract with the manufacturer. So how could he sue directly to recover damages caused by the defective car? The manufacturer stood in a special relationship—called privity of contract—with the retailer. The relationship was an impediment to recovery. But Cardozo reasoned that for purposes of tort law, the relationship was not limited to the contract of sale. The manufacturer also has a relevant relationship with the consumer. If the manufacturer was negligent relative to the plaintiff-consumer, then it also violated its duty of care. Imposing liability against the manufacturer was thought, at the time, to be a major breakthrough in legal thought.

The curious thing is that in *Palsgraf*, the victim has a direct contractual relationship with the railroad. She had bought a ticket for her children and herself to Rockaway Beach. She stood in privity with the Long Island Railroad Company and they owed her a duty of care. Nonetheless Cardozo saw the issue of duty as a way of overriding the judgment of liability to the plaintiff. He returns to the problem that haunted Blackstone in *Scott v Shepherd*. Whom is

---

[32] *MacPherson v Buick*, 217 NY 382 (1916).

the tort committed against? Is it a wrong against a specific party or a wrong against the society as a whole? We referred to these earlier as the private law and public law theories of tort liability. There was no doubt that Cardozo, like Blackstone before him, was on the side of tort law as private law.

Here are some of the eloquent phrases in which he expresses this idea (in many of these instances he is quoting other judges):

— 'In every instance, before negligence can be predicated of a given act, back of the act must be sought and found a duty to the individual complaining, the observance of which would have averted or avoided the injury';[33]
— 'The ideas of negligence and duty are strictly correlative';[34]
— 'The plaintiff sues in her own right for a wrong personal to her, and not as the vicarious beneficiary of a breach of duty to another'.[35]

He sums up by stressing the fundamental difference between crime and tort. In crime the duty is owed to the public; in tort it is owed to the specific person injured.

We should remember, however, that Judge Andrews was on the other side—as were the majority of the judges on the King's Bench in 1773. There is no right or wrong on this issue. Sometimes the view of torts as private law holds sway. Sometimes the conception of negligence as unlawful action—a wrong to the public—dominates.

As applied to the *Palsgraf* case the theory of duty—a pre-eminently legal, not factual issue—provides the basis for overturning the verdicts. According to Cardozo, the judge should never have sent the case to the jury. Why? Because, as he surmised, the men who jostled the passenger boarding the train owed no duty of care to Ms Palsgraf? Why not? They were indeed negligent in handling the package. Why did they owe no duty to the person directly injured by the blast? Cardozo's key line to resolve this issue is 'the eye of reasonable vigilance'. As he sums up:

> If no hazard was apparent to the eye of ordinary vigilance, an act innocent and harmless, at least to outward seeming, with reference to her,

[33] Quoted from *W Va Central R Co v State*, 96 Md 652 at 666 (19xx) (per McSherry J).
[34] Quoted from *Thomas v Quartermaine*, 18 QBD 685 at 694 (per Bowen LJ).
[35] Quoted from *Palsgraf* at 342.

did not take to itself the quality of a tort because it happened to be a wrong ... with reference to some one else.[36]

There, a tort against the man boarding the train was not a tort against Ms Palsgraf. The person of reasonable vigilance could not have anticipated the explosion that would rock the scales on the other side of the station. Although the Railroad owed her a duty of care, they were not liable, derivatively, for the agents' torts having been committed against the man boarding the train. Note that nominally Cardozo's opinion is not about the concept of probable cause. It is about the basic elements of tort liability, one of them being a duty of care to the specific person injured in the accident. If we were to apply Cardozo's standard of duty to the cases we have considered so far we should have to predict their outcomes as follows:

Scott v Shepherd: liability, one could expect that the lit bomb would endanger people all over the market
Brown v Kendall: no liability, no expectation that plaintiff might be standing behind the defendant.
Rylands v Fletcher: no liability, no expectation and therefore no duty to neighbouring landowner.
Polemis: no liability, no expectation of harm to those injured by the explosion.

Of course, there might be disagreement about these predictions because it is difficult to predict how far 'the eye of reasonable vigilance' will cast its net.

Justice Andrews argued the issue differently: 'where there is an act that unreasonably threatens the interests of others, is the doer liable for all the proximate consequences?'[37] He gives the example of driving down Broadway at a reckless speed. This is negligence—without specifying a duty to the specific person who might be injured. It is a wrong to the public—precisely the idea that Cardozo tried to avoid in defining negligence. For Andrews, the critical question was not whether there was negligence, but whether a negligent act is found by the jury to be the proximate cause of the damages.

---

[36] *Ibid.*
[37] *Ibid* at 347.

Note that duty is a question of law. If the jury decides under the wrong instruction concerning duty, they can be reversed. Proximate cause is a question of fact. According to Andrews' opinion, the jury had decided that the act proximately caused the injuries; this should have been the end of the matter.

Cardozo's opinion is read widely but whether it has had much influence on the law is subject to debate. The thrust of the opinion is to overcome the view that an act is negligence because it threatens the public interest in general. An act is supposedly negligence only if it can be expected—by 'the eye of reasonable vigilance'—to invade the particular interests of the particular plaintiff. Yet the debate about tort law as public (because negligence threatens the public) or private (but it is the violation of the interests of the particular plaintiff) is far from over. As we see in the next chapter, the school of law and economics has vigorously defended the view that risks should be considered negligence when they violate the interests of the public as a whole.

Palsgraf laid the seeds for a major transformation of our thinking about proximate cause. Cardozo's modification of *Polemis* was that the holding was limited to liability for damage to the ship. It could not extend to 'an *unforeseeable* invasion of an interest of another order, as, eg, one of bodily security'.[38]

The word 'unforeseeable' became the lynchpin of modern approaches to proximate cause. Eventually, it became the binding standard in the United Kingdom[39] as well as the United States and other common law countries. Not surprisingly, the same word, translated appropriately, has a grip on the minds of French and German lawyers as well.[40]

The standard of unforeseeability has this appeal even though every sophisticated law student knows that it is subject to infinite

---

[38] *Ibid* at 346–7.

[39] In the UK the concept of foreseeability was further refined in the landmark cases of *Wagon Mound I (Overseas Tankship (UK) Ltd v Morts Dock & Eng'g Co* [1961] AC 388 (PC) and *Wagon Mound II (Overseas Tankship (UK) Ltd v Miller SS Co* [1967] AC 617).

[40] Dalloz, *Code Civil*, 12th edn, eds G Goubeaux, P Bihr and X Henry (1997–98) at 1071, fn 41 (relying on the word *imprevisible*). The term *Voraussehbarkeit* is generally used in the German literature but not always: see *Muenchner Kommentar, Buergetiches Gesetzbuch: Schuldrecht: Allgemeiner Teil*, ed W Krueger (2003), Commentary to §. 249, pp 328–34 (explaining the *Adaequanztheorie* and other theories of proximate cause).

manipulation. The more precisely a result is described, the less foreseeable it is. The more broadly it is defined, the more foreseeable. It was surely foreseeable that Shepherd's throwing the bomb would injure someone in the market but it was presumably not foreseeable that it would injure Scott in the eye. Yet for all its vagueness and imprecision, the standard of foreseeability bears a close connection to the fault standard and, in particular, as we shall see, to the cost–benefit analysis of fault. If risk-takers are to be held liable because they choose an undesirable risk over the benefits of an alternative mode of conduct, then their liability should extend no further than the boundaries of the risk as it was knowable or foreseeable to them. This makes sense for the fault standard, but it is not at all self-evident that we should apply the same standard in cases of intentional torts or strict liability.

The conventional way to approach the problem of proximate cause is to treat the issue as the second stage of a two-part doctrine of causation. The first stage is usually called 'cause-in-fact': the question whether the harmful event would have happened anyway or whether the alleged negligence of the defendant was the condition 'but for which the result would not have occurred'. This famous 'sine qua non' test is used around the world, but as I will show later, there are many issues of causation that this test ignores and it may in fact apply in actual cases in a very limited number of situations. The entire field of causation was brilliantly re-evaluated in the book by HLA Hart and Tony Honore.[41] They exposed the fallacies in the 'sine qua non' test and challenged the reliance of the courts on the test of 'foreseeability' as the criterion of proximate cause. We will revisit this problems in chapter three, where we examine the larger context of the paradigm of liability of which they are a part.

5. COMPARATIVE ANALYSIS

The torts systems of the Western industrialised societies are similarly structured with many superficial similarities. Whether they are 'codified' or not, they all break down their systems according

---

[41] Hart and Honore, *Causation in the Law*, 2nd edn (Oxford, Clarendon Press, 1985).

to intentional torts, negligence, and strict liability. There are some differences with regard to the possibility of expanding strict liability by judicial decision. German courts have a fixed category of *Gefährdungshaftung* (strict liability for risky activities). These legislative provisions are largely outside the Code and function, more or less, like workers' compensation plans. In France, as well as the English-speaking countries, the line between strict liability and fault is subject to judicial control and reinterpretation. The best provision for imposing strict liability resembles Blackburn's principle in *Rylands v Fletcher*. According to section 1384 of the *Code Civil*, if you have something in your charge that might escape and do harm, you are liable for the consequences. On its face this is a principle of strict liability—standing in contrast to section 1382, which provides: '*Tout fait quelconque de l'homme, qui cause à autrui un dommage, oblige celui par la faute duquel il est arrivé, à le reparer.*' ['Every action of a person that causes damage to another imposes an obligation of repair on the person whose fault the action is.']

Daringly, in 1930 the Cour de Cassation extended the strict liability principle of section 1384 to motor vehicle accidents.[42] The car was considered a thing under the driver's control. If it escaped and did damage, liability attached. The only exceptions were variations of *force majeure*. If the driver could show that a gunman forced him to make the fatal turn, he would be exempt. The same principle applies in the *Rylands* line of cases. As the Exchequer Chamber added in *Rylands*: the defendant could excuse himself by 'showing that the escape was owing to the plaintiff's default, or, perhaps, that the escape was the consequence of *vis major* or the act of God'.[43] This is an important modification, for it shows that neither in French law nor common law is strict liability equivalent to absolute liability. There is always an opportunity to show that the action is excused if the defendant was not responsible for the risk.

The 1930 decision of the French court reveals the active participation of the courts and the doctrinal writers in the development of French tort law. No one could solve a legal problem—say, liability for infecting another person with the AIDS virus—just on the basis

---

[42] Case of *Jend'heur*, Cour de Cassation, Chambres réunies, 13 February 1930, Dalloz 1930.I.57. On French opinions including this leading case, see Michael with 'French and American Judicial Opinions' (1994)19 *Yale Law Journal* 84.

[43] *Rylands v Fletcher* (1868) LR 3 HL 330.

of this language of the French Code or any other code. Elaboration by the courts and the scholar is always necessary. The basic reference tool for French lawyers, the Dalloz edition of the *Code Civil*, contained as of a few years ago 14 pages of fine print on the meaning of the elements of liability, including several paragraphs on whether the loss of an opportunity or the imposition of a risk of AIDS constitutes 'damage' for the purposes of tort liability. This commentary consists of 99 distinct paragraphs, and each paragraph relies on a judicial decision or a scholarly article.

It is important to distinguish two variations of the proposition that the civilian codes determine all cases in advance. One view is that the code actually dictates the result of particular cases, something in the same way as algorithms determine the electronic responses of a computer. This naive conception of the statutory law is expressed in the metaphor coined by Baron de Montesquieu that the judge is merely '*la bouche de la loi*' ['the mouthpiece of the law'].[44] No one who has actually tried to solve a problem of tort liability using the few words devoted to torts in the *Code Civil* could possibly hold this view.

The more sophisticated version of the argument that a code in the Continental tradition determines the outcome of all disputes is that the code prescribes the concepts and the terminology for thinking about all legal disputes. This is also not true. Consider the problem of the plaintiff's negligence in tort cases. This is called contributory or comparative negligence, and we take up the issue in chapter three. The French *Code Civil* of 1804 says nothing about this problem— either about the rule or the terminology for discussing the problem. The courts invented the phrase *faute commune* [shared fault or, more literally, communal fault] for assaying the matter, but this term in itself does not inform us whether the guiding rule should be comparative or contributory negligence. One might expect a modernised version of the 1804 French *Code Civil* to address this problem. But even in the 1994 revision of the Quebec Civil Code (said to be faithful to 'civil law' tradition) there is no reference to contributory or comparative negligence, but Article 1478 seems to adapt aportionment to include the victim's duty to pay on the basic of fault.

---

[44] Charles de Secondat, Baron de Montesquieu, *The Spirit of Laws*, Book 11b, Chapter 6 (1748): 'The national judges are no more than the mouth that pronounces the words of the law, mere passive beings, incapable of moderating either its force or rigour.'

The German Civil Code of 1900 (abbreviated to BGB) is no more successful than the French Code of 1804 in addressing and resolving all problems that might arise in private law litigation. Unlike the French Code, the German Code did have a very finely drafted provision on comparative fault by the plaintiff.[45] And perhaps the original plan was to encompass all issues that might arise in private litigation. Shortly after the BGB came into force, however, a scholar noticed that the provisions of the Code provided no answer for the case of a negligent contractual breach that results in physical damage to the other party.[46] A good example would be medical malpractice or a defective product resulting in harm. These problems could be handled as torts under the BGB but there were good reasons for approaching them as problems of contract rather than tort, one primary reason being the advantages of holding principals liable for the actions of their agents. Contract law recognises the principle of strict vicarious liability—see BGB section 278—but tort liability requires that the principal be negligent in the selection or supervision of the agent who unlawfully causes harm (BGB section 831). The rule on agency liability provides an incentive for medical malpractice plaintiffs to classify their case as a matter of contract rather than tort.

To extend the scope of contractual liability to cover these cases, the scholars invented two doctrines now well known in other civil law countries. One is called '*culpa in contrahendo*'—that is, fault in the process of making a contract. And the other is termed 'positive breach of contract'—which the common law and French law seem to have had all along. Since then these concepts have been absorbed into German law as standard categories of contractual liability. Quite recently, in 2002, the German Parliament amended the Code to incorporate the new doctrines in BGB section 280,[47] although they had been recognised as 'law' by the courts and the literature for at least a hundred years.

Despite their relative cultural isolation, French, German, and US tort law have all developed in a similar fashion. They all divide

---

[45] BGB §254.

[46] Hermann Staub, *Die positiven Vertragsverletzungen und ihre Rechtsfolgen* (Berlin, T Guttentag, 1902).

[47] 'If the obligor fails to comply with a duty arising under the obligation, the obligee may claim compensation for the loss resulting from this breach. This does not apply if the obligor is not liable for the failure': BGB §280(1).

the system into intentional torts, negligence, and strict liability. They all recognise the relevance of the plaintiff's fault as a factor bearing on liability. They all use the same tests and language for determining cause in fact (the sine qua non test) and proximate cause (foreseeability). They have all had sufficient internal flexibility to recognise the right to privacy (or right to personality, as it is formulated on the Continent) as a new tort protected by their civil codes. Yet there are two differences—one small and one huge—that are worth keeping in mind. We consider the minor difference now and the huge one in Section 7 below.

The tendency in Continental practice is to move the boundary between tort and crime to include more cases of contract and fewer of tort. This is important for Continental lawyers to realise when they turn to issues under the ATCA. They may think of product liability and medical malpractice as contract disputes, but the Americans instinctively classify these as torts. Until recently, it was very unusual for there to be a special course on torts in European and Latin American law schools. The subject was typically assumed under the law of obligations, also covering contracts and unjust enrichment.

6. IF CRIMINAL, TORT FOLLOWS

A general doctrine recognised in Western systems of tort law is that a violation of a criminal or regulatory standard that protects particular individuals entails tort liability for the damage done. This doctrine is called 'negligence per se' in the common law.[48] The unexcused violation of the regulatory standard generates a directed verdict for tort liability in negligence. Yet the doctrine is not limited to negligence cases. The German BGB section 823(II) states the principle more broadly: Any violation of a law designed to protect others is considered a sufficient basis for liability. If fault is required under the protective law, it is also required for tort liability. The United States has adopted an analogous provision for violations of the Constitution. Under the *Bivens* principle, the violation of a constitutional right, say, under the Fourth Amendment

---

[48] See Restatement of the Law (Third), Torts: Liability for Physical Harm (Basic Principles) §14 Statutory 'Violations as Negligence Per Se' (2001).

against unreasonable searches and seizures, generates a right to compensation for injury, in effect, a tort based on violation of the Constitution.[49]

These various doctrines, negligence per se and *Bivens*, provide a guide to the intepretation of the ATCA. The violation of an international law designed to protect individuals should result in tort liability for the damage done. It is a familiar principle in Western tort law. We need only render more precise the kinds of international violations that qualify for liability. That will follow in due course. Of immediate concern, however, is recognising the way the US tort system differs radically from the civilian model.

7. PUNITIVE DAMAGES

The huge difference between the Continental and the common law systems of tort law is the system of incentives for lawyers, including the topic now to be examined: punitive damages in the English-speaking world. When the prospect of billion-dollar recoveries is added to the jury system, and lawyers are permitted to work on the contingency fee system (taking one-third of the recovery instead of an hourly fee), the engine of tort liability suddenly finds enormous traction. The incentives to sue large, solvent defendants for human rights abuses in violation of the ATCA are overwhelming. The lynchpin of this engine is the principle of punitive damages. Why we have this institution, how we justify it, how we control it—all of this requires considerable discussion.

Punitive damages are rooted in the initially overlapping relationship between trespass as a tort and trespass as a crime. As early the thirteenth century various enactments provided for double, treble, or quadruple damages. These provisions obviously reveal the influence of the book of Exodus, which generated a highly complicated scheme of punitive damages. For example, in the case of stealing, slaughtering, and selling the carcass of an animal, the obligation was to repay five oxen for an ox and four sheep for a sheep.[50] Other provisions recognised the duty to pay double damages.[51] As

---

[49] *Bivens v Six Unknown Federal Narcotics Agents*, 403 US 388 (1971).
[50] Exodus 21:37.
[51] Exodus 22:3 (if stolen goods are found in the possession of the thief).

we have seen, however, trespass evolved toward Case and sought to free itself of its original criminal overtones of trespass *vi et armis*. It abandoned the principle of liability for directly causing harm, even though the standard of 'direct harm' long survived in other areas of the law. Yet the unified law of tort retained the provision of punitive damages in order to punish those defendants who, in the court's view, deserved it.

The Fifth and Sixth Amendments to the US Constitution require certain procedural protections in all 'criminal prosecutions'. Among these are the principles of double jeopardy and the privilege against self-incrimination. The standard view is that these constitutional rights do not extend to tort disputes; they apply only in criminal cases. Yet the test for whether a case is criminal is whether it imposes punishment,[52] and punitive damages seem clearly to impose punishment. Yet surprisingly, in tort cases, juries and courts have retained the power to punish defendants in a way totally inconsistent with Sixth Amendment jurisprudence. The power to punish by imposing heavy damage awards—with funds going not to the state but to the plaintiff—is one of the distinguishing features of the common law of torts. No Continental system follows this practice. For the purposes of alien tort claims, the possibility of punitive damages should be the first consideration motivating the lawyer for the plaintiff.

In the second half of the twentieth century, courts developed various techniques for controlling excessive verdicts of juries. Judges assert the power of *remittitur*[53] to reduce the amount of jury verdicts. Significantly, however, the courts never tried to take away the power of juries to assess punitive damages. In criminal cases, judges assumed the power to determine sentences—the criminal law analogue to the level of damages—but they never tried to do the same in civil cases. It is an open question whether they could have succeeded under the Seventh Amendment, which guarantees the right to a jury trial in all 'suits at common law'.

[52] *Kennedy v Mendoza-Martinez*, 372 US 144 (1963).

[53] *Remittitur* is the procedural process by which an excessive verdict by the jury is reduced. If money damages awarded by a jury are grossly excessive as a matter of law, the judge may order the plaintiff to remit a portion of the award. In the alternative, the court may order a complete new trial or a trial limited to the issues of damages. The court may also condition a denial of a motion for new trial upon the filing by the plaintiff of a *remittitur* in a stated amount: *Black's Law Dictionary*, 6th edn (pub details, 1990) at 1295.

It is much easier for judges to intervene on questions of substantive law than to challenge the power of common law juries. For example, in an important decision in 1964, the court decided for the first time that the First Amendment protecting freedom of speech applied on behalf of the *New York Times* against an allegedly defamed police commissioner in Montgomery, Alabama.[54] The state court had granted an award of a half million dollars in damages for both compensatory and punitive damages. The court could have set aside the award for punitive damages on the ground that it was arbitrary and a violation of due process, but the justices did not dare mention the issue. They found it more convenient to issue a broad and radical ruling defending the freedom of the press and restricting liability for defamation against public officials.

Beginning in the early 1990s, however, the Supreme Court began to test both the power of juries to fix punitive damages and that of judges to enter orders of *remittitur* to control the damage awards. They proceeded slowly and tentatively. In the first few decisions they discussed the constitutional aspects of excessive awards but they did not reverse the rulings of the state courts.[55] The relevant constitutional provisions were the prohibition against 'excessive fines' in the Eighth Amendment and the general requirement of due process under the Fourteenth Amendment.

Finally, in 1996, the court received a case in which the facts were sufficiently convincing to warrant intervention. Interestingly, this was another case appealed from the apparently generous pattern of decisions by Alabama juries.

Dr Ira Gore was a very particular consumer. He bought a new black BMW sports sedan in Birmingham. After driving it for nine months he wanted to make it look even 'snazzier' so he took it, believe it or not, to a point shop called 'Slick Finish'. Upon examining the car, Mr Slick detected evidence that the car had already been repainted in part. Crestfallen, Ira took his complaint to the BMW dealer, who informed him that BMW had a policy of fixing minor defects caused by production or shipping without telling the

---

[54] *Sullivan v New York Times*, 376 US 254 (1964).
[55] The first case was *Pacific Mutual Life Ins Co v Haslip*, 499 US 1 (1991) (damage award of over $1 million to plaintiff on the grounds that the insurance agent had fraudulent diverted the payment of premiums on the policy; the punitive portion of the award was $800,000).

customer. 'Minor' was defined as being worth less than 3% of the retail price. Repainting the relevant portion of Gore's car cost $601 or about 1.5% of the retail price.

Gore decided to sue. He asked for $500,000 in compensatory damages but the jury was not willing to award more than $4,000 based on the reduction of price BMW experienced when they revealed the defects and sold the cars as used. The issue on appeal was not the $4,000 but an additional award of four million dollars in punitive damages. The jury had found that the BMW policy satisfied the statutory requirement of 'gross, oppressive, or malicious' fraud. But the numbers seemed over the top—500 times the figure Gore deserved to compensate him for his damages. The Alabama state court had imposed a *remittitur* and reduced the amount to two million. On appeal to the Supreme Court, the defendant argued that even this sum was irrational and a violation of due process.

The court had few tools to work with. How could it define an appropriate relationship between the compensatory award and the punitive judgment? On the one hand, if it set a specific number—say, punitive four or five times compensatory—it would seem just as arbitrary as the biblical rule on stealing oxen and sheep. On the other hand, it could not intervene and reverse a state court judgment without providing some guidance for the future.

For example, one of the ways that Gore's lawyers were able to convince the jury to award four million dollars (even an Alabama jury needs some convincing) was to claim to represent the victims of the BMW policy all over the country. The Alabama Supreme Court reduced the award on the ground that it was inappropriate for Alabama to punish BMW dealers around the country. The US Supreme Court underscored that, under principles of federalism, 'each State has ample power to protect its own consumers, [but] none may use the punitive damages deterrent as a means of imposing its regulatory policies on the entire Nation'.[56]

This is a justifiable limitation on punitive damages, but labelling 'punitive damages' as a 'deterrent' opens the door to much higher damage awards, particularly in the case of large, well-funded defendants who are not so easily deterred by monetary damages. Economists have long taught us that corporations can simply write

[56] *BMW of North America v Gore*, 517 US 559 (1996) at 586.

off damage awards as a 'cost of doing business'. The temptation would be to argue that the richer a corporation is, the higher the award should be in order to achieve a satisfactory deterrent.

To a conventional tort lawyer—unfamiliar with the inner workings of punitive damages—this is a shocking argument. The entire principle of corrective justice, as proposed by Aristotle, is based on the idea that the function of tort law should be only to repair the loss in the particular transaction.[57] The purpose should not be distributive justice, which is designed to achieve a just distribution of assets across the entire society. Thus, it would be unthinkable, in an ordinary tort case, to reason that a richer defendant should pay more just because he or she was rich. Of course, lawyers always seek defendants with 'deep pockets', but in principle they are not allowed to introduce evidence either about defendants' insurance policies or their balance sheets.

Yet once we move from the realm of corrective to punitive justice, just about anything is possible. In one of its early cases in the field, the Supreme Court actually said that a large punitive award was justifiable in light of the defendant's 'wealth'.[58] The entire Supreme Court seems to accept the idea that 'deterrence' is one of the proper goals of punitive damages, and if this is true, then perhaps it does follow that a richer defendant should be hit with a larger damage award.

In a recent case of a smoker who sued Philip Morris in Oregon for engaging in fraudulent misrepresentation of the carcinogenic dangers of cigarettes,[59] three parties in Oregon wrestled with the question of the appropriate amount of compensatory and punitive damages—the jury, the trial judge, and the state court of appeals. They all took different views. The numbers came out this way.

	Economic Losses	Non-economic Losses[60]	Punitive Damages
Jury	$21,485.80	$800,000.00	$79,500,000.00
Trial Judge	same	$500,000.00	$32,000,000.00
Appellate Court	same	same	$79,500,000.00

---

[57] See Weinrib, above n 19.

[58] *TXO Productions v Alliance Resources*, 409 US 443–2 (1993) at 461. Cf *Haslip*, above n 55 ('financial condition' relevant).

[59] *Williams v Philip Morris*, 92 P.3d 126 (2004).

[60] These include pain and suffering and other dignitary interests.

In other words, on the basis of current principles of the Supreme Court,[61] the Oregon appellate court thought it appropriate to reverse the trial judge's *remittitur* and reinstate the jury's verdict of $79.5 million. Not only did the court affirm the relevance of Philip Morris's wealth but it indulged in another dubious assumption about the relevant criteria for determining punitive damages: It could award damages to the plaintiff on the basis of injuries to other smokers within the state. Consider: 'The jury also could have found that Williams was one of thousands of Oregonians who received the defendant's message, acted on it, and like him, suffered cancer or other diseases as a result.'[62] The court guessed that there were probably 100 smokers who were influenced by the defendant's claim that the scientific evidence about the effects of smoking was inconclusive. The plaintiff was allowed to collect for all of them.

Allowing punitive damages to the plaintiff because of hypothetical other parties in a similar situation represents an injustice both to the defendant and to those unrepresented hypothetical parties who will never receive a share of the $79.5 million awarded to the plaintiff's family.

Worse than the injustice (depending on your perspective) is the logical incoherence of both the background Supreme Court decisions and their application in this Oregon case. The official policy of the courts is to permit jury instructions that emphasise both the punitive nature of the award and the desirability of deterring future bad conduct. In the *Gore* decision, the court outlined the elements of the punitive side of the judgment. The most important factor is the 'reprehensible conduct' of the defendant. There is no doubt that Philip Morris's behaviour was more reprehensible than BMW's. Therefore, it deserved greater punishment—but how much greater the punishment should be remains in the jury's discretion. That they were allowed to consider harm to another 100 hypothetical victims strains credulity. In a criminal case, the defendant's other

---

[61] The leading case at the time was *State Farm Mutual Ins v Campbell*, 538 US 408 (2003). The court held that the measure of punishment must be both reasonable and proportionate to the amount of harm to the plaintiff and to the general damages recovered. They overturned a punitive damage amount of $145 million when compensatory damages were only $1 million.

[62] *Williams v Philip Morris* at 130.

crimes would not be relevant for sentencing unless they could be satisfactorily established in the sentencing hearing. Here the jury was allowed to guess about the number of other victims, and worse than that, award this plaintiff for 'reprehensible conduct' towards them.

That is not all. Retribution is about the past. Punishing is for the sake of the victims and the imperative to do justice. Deterrence addresses the future. How much should the award sting the defendants to ensure that they and other companies will not do it (or anything like it) ever again. In this context, the wealth of the defendant becomes a relevant factor, serving as well to augment the punitive award.

Whether these decisions on punitive damages are correct or not, they are of the highest importance in suits for human rights abuses. In violations of international law—as in cases of torture, killing of civilians, war crimes, and crimes against humanity—the actions of the defendant are obviously reprehensible. The evil perpetrated by Philip Morris is relatively minor compared with the large-scale abuses of human rights that we witness around the world. When these abuses can be properly framed for law suits under the ATCA, the law of punitive damages will shape the size of jury awards.

Quite remarkably, there does not seem to be a developed case-law under the ATCA about the permissibility and appropriate scope of punitive damages. The reason might be that cases arise on a motion to dismiss before the jury has had a chance to assess damages. As with most issues under the ATCA, however, there might be room for defendants to argue that the matter should be governed by the law of nations and that punitive damages do not exist in the law of nations. This form of argument is ventured on various occasions, including whether corporations can be liable for aiding and abetting the primary human rights offenders.[63] In the end the argument has little traction, largely because it is well recognised that international law addresses the general principles of liability and leaves the modes of enforcement to the nation states. In addition, under the ATCA, liability in tort implies liability according to the established institutions of tort law, including the major factors that create financial incentives in the US tort system.

---

[63] This is taken up in ch 7.

There is another lesson we should derive from the recent history of punitive damages. For all the arguments that we find that tort law is private law, the institution of punitive damages remains a constant reminder that the institution serves the public purposes of deterrence and social reform. The courts can no longer say whether a smoker's claim for lung cancer is just about him or her or whether it is about the entire issues of smoking and public health. And what about Gore and his new BMW? How does his personal grievance get transformed into a medium for changing the pricing practices of an entire industry? Tort law becomes the vehicle for solving and regulating large social problems by coercing industrial actors—through large-scale jury verdicts—into acting properly in the public interest. It is not surprising, then, that in the last 25 years the ATCA has also become a vehicle for correcting human rights abuses that occur around the world.

Yet tort theory is torn by contradictions. How can courts say that the policy of tort law is both corrective justice and deterrence of future wrongs, both about compensating for past wrongs and preventing future harm? Can a single suit be guided both by the damages that have occurred to the plaintiff and by the overall wealth of the defendant? No lawyer should dare go near this explosive field of law without knowledge of the theoretical conflicts that lie beneath the law and which are never fully addressed in the opinions of the courts. Only by explicating these conflicting theoretical approaches can we possibility understand the forces at play in these decisions.

My approach to this problem is to explicate conflicting paradigms of liability, each of which is coherent in itself and becomes problematic only when it must coexist in the legal culture with the alternative paradigms. Thus we proceed in the next three chapters to explore three archetypes or models of tort liability the paradigms of economic analysis, of reciprocity, and of aggression.

2

The Paradigm of Efficiency

In the leading law schools of the United States, the dominant language for analysing tort liability and most other fields of law is the idiom of efficiency and cost–benefit analysis, as developed in the school of law and economics (L&E). Except for a few judges who have come to the bench from academia (and these primarily from the University of Chicago), the language of economics has not yet penetrated the thinking of the courts. Nonetheless, the language of efficiency and cost–benefit analysis cannot be ignored. It is an entrenched part of US legal thought and rapidly gaining influence abroad.

My approach to this entire school is critical—but not dismissive. It is important to study the origins of L&E in tort law, not only to understand the opposition but to express respect for the subtle intellectual manoeuvres that have led to the ascendancy of L&E.

When we speak of the influence of the economists, we have to distinguish radically between the free market enthusiasts, typified by Friedrich Hayek and Milton Freedman, and the utilitarian balancers, who trace their roots primarily to Jeremy Bentham in the eighteenth century. The difference between these two schools is fundamental. The followers of Hayek are committed to individual liberty and oppose governmental intervention based on the judgement of officials about what is good for society. The followers of Bentham are just the opposite: they are in favour of governmental intervention based on the judgement of judges and other officials about what is good for the general welfare. Yet both sides of the aisle use the same language of efficiency. This should put us on our guard when we see claims about the efficiency of legal arrangements. The internal contradiction is reminiscent of the two different ways that Kant uses the term 'freedom'. Negative freedom means freedom from restraint, the freedom to do whatever you choose to do. Positive freedom refers to the freedom to do the right things as dictated by your duty and the principles of morality.[1]

Economists would be well advised, for the sake of clarity, to distinguish in a like manner between negative and positive efficiency. Negative efficiency means that when every producer and consumer is allowed to act freely in the marketplace, the market will reach the best results for everyone. Positive efficiency enters the analysis when for various reasons the market is not able to work perfectly, and governmental officials intervene in the market to achieve that which they think people would choose if they could. This most typically occurs when a judge or official makes a cost–benefit analysis and imposes it on the society in the name of efficiency. In order to make a cost–benefit judgement, however, judges must assume that there is a common denominator by which they can measure the conflicting goods. The utilitarians claimed that they could compare the units of utility gained by one person with the units of disutility suffered by another. Free markets theories railed against this assumption of a common denominator and insisted that the market was the only proper mechanism for measuring efficiency: only by actually observing their choices can we know what preferences people have and what choices they want to make.

The basic problem of tort law in the marketplace is that the process of buying and selling cannot in itself generate duties to compensate persons who are injured in the course of these trades. Of course, the market can generate private insurance policies, and sometimes it does that either by seeking insurance policies or by tacking on a specific insurance programme to the sale of a dangerous commodity. For example, not long ago French ski slopes sold two tickets. At the lower price you received no compensation for injuries received in the course of skiing. At the higher you were completely covered. Insurance policies would eliminate many of the problems of tort law—at least for routine injuries.

Human rights abuses are not routine. Whether someone is poisoned in a ground war, raped in wartime, or tortured in a foreign country,

---

[1] For an analagous distinciton see Isaiah Berlin, *Two Concepts of Liberty* (Oxford, The Clarendon Press, 1958) (supporting negative as opposed to positive liberty).

each event stands out as an event that requires individual analysis and correction. These are not events to be considered under the lens of 'efficient' social management. The economic analysis of law may ultimately have no bearing on our specific subject but it is worth considering in case the contrary argument is made (and I expect that eventually it will be made).[2]

1. THE TRANSITION FROM NEGATIVE TO POSITIVE EFFICIENCY

Imagine that the goods of society are distributed to the members of society in a more or less equal way. Yet the goods are different. Some people have television sets, others have shoes, others have sugar, and still others, tobacco. As life begins in this imaginary society, the players realise that they have different goods. The one with shoes realises that he would like a TV set, and the possessor of the televisions senses immediately that she would like some shoes. The two of them consider a trade and begin negotiating. Eventually they will agree on a 'price' for the TV set in the currency of shoes, say five pairs of shoes for one 19-inch colour set. The two parties exchange the goods. The exchange is based on consent, freely given, informed by knowledge of all the available alternatives.

Economists now assume that both parties are better off as a result of the trade. Otherwise, they say, they would have no incentive for making the trade. The party who gets the shoes values five pairs of shoes more than she values a television set. The party who gets the TV set prefers it to five pairs of shoes. Their 'utilities', viewed subjectively, are enhanced.

The trade makes the world better off, insofar as it makes at least one of the parties better off and it makes no one worse off. Now note what happens when the possessor of tobacco wants to trade his stock for a TV set. He goes to a TV owner and offers her an amount of tobacco. She responds that she despises tobacco and

---

[2] There is a similar problem as to whether the defence of lesser evils—a variation of the principle of efficiency—as formulated in Rome Statute, Art 31(1)(d) applies in cases of genocide, war crimes, and crimes against humanity. This problem has not received the theoretical attention it deserves. For further analysis on this point, see pp 129–30 below.

that in fact you would have to pay her to take it. What should the tobacco holder do? He has two ways of obtaining a TV set. He can search around for other parties who are willing to trade something for tobacco (shoes will work, or possibly sugar) that he can use to entice the TV holder into selling a TV set. Or he can wait until someone who likes tobacco comes into possession of a TV set. The world would be much simpler for the tobacco holder if everyone used an intermediate, common commodity that everyone liked. That common denominator is called money. If they had a common currency—say, dollars—everyone would trade first for dollars, then use the dollars to buy what they really wanted.

This model of economic relations assumes ignorance about the quantitative extent of the gain from each trade. We know that when the shoe holder and the TV possessor trade, each makes himself/herself better off. But we do not know how much better off each becomes. Nor can we say whether one gains more than the other. The reason for this limitation is that utility in economics is entirely subjective. It depends on how much individuals are actually willing to pay for the goods they want. This ignorance about relative gain induced economists to recognise that their principle of efficiency was merely negative and not positive. Another way to put this is that they refused to address the *interpersonal comparison of utilities*. The most we can do is derive a map of utilities for each person, and that map is based on the choices he or she actually makes.

As it stands, this pure version of the market could not possibly be of relevance to the law—except in the rare cases suggested by the French ski slope tickets. Its underlying principle is the sovereignty and autonomy of every player in the market. The market is voluntary; its supreme principle is consent. But the law is coercive. The market depends on decentralised, uncoordinated decisions, but the law stands for centralised decision-making. In order to achieve relevance to lawyers and policy-makers, the system of Pareto efficiency had to undergo a transformation that would enable it to appeal to partisans of coercive intervention and positive efficiency. How this transformation occurred is the tale we now tell.

First we should clarify the meaning of Pareto efficiency in the narrow sense. Trading is Pareto efficient when any trade will result in a subjectively better condition for at least one of the parties. The other party feels no worse off and his or her partner feels better off. A Pareto optimal situation is a state of standstill—no further trades are possible. No one can change his or her position without feeling worse off. The important premise of the system is that it is entirely empirical. The only way you know whether a trade is Pareto superior is to observe whether the two real-life people will actually make the trade. It is assumed that in these traditional situations the parties have full information on the options for trade and there are no impediments to their making the trade they would like to make.

The beginnings of the transformation of the Pareto standard took hold in the late 1930s when a British economist, Nicholas Kaldor, turned his mind to a problem that national legislatures have often confronted.[3] May they make a legislative change that will benefit the economy as a whole even if the change implies that a certain group in the society will lose? The specific problem was the nineteenth-century debate in Britain about the Corn Laws, the protective tariffs that shielded British farmers from foreign competition. A similar debate occurred recently in the United States about joining the North American Free Trade Association (NAFTA). Participating in the tariff reduction programme of NAFTA might be good for the country as a whole but certain producers would lose out to cheaper Mexican imports.

Kaldor argued that the gains from free trade to the country as a whole were likely to be sufficiently great to outweigh the loss to some corn farmers. Kaldor believed that the winners could have purchased the right to remove the tariffs from the farmers and still have gains left over. The possibility of that buy-out justified the imposition of the Corn Laws without an actual buy-out, which would have been impractical in light of the number of parties. Another economist, John Hicks, quickly extended the argument to all market impediments.[4] Whenever someone would buy an interest in the market (but cannot because of impediments in the market), and the state forces the transaction, the result is efficient. That is, it would be negatively efficient if the purchaser actually bought the interest. But the voluntary trade never occurs. The state intervenes

---

[3] Nicholas Kaldor, 'Welfare Propositions of Economics and Interpersonal Comparisons of Utility', (1939) 49 *Economics Journal* 549.
[4] John Hicks, 'The Foundations of Welfare Economics', (1939) 49 *Economics Journal* 696.

on the assumption that the trade would be negatively efficient. Thus negative efficiency—which is supposed to exist exclusively in the free market—becomes an argument for state intervention in the economy.

It is sometimes said that hard cases make bad law, and this is an instance in which an easy economic problem (abolishing restraints on free trade) generated a dubious moral principle. Kaldor's and Hicks' ruminations about the Corn Laws transformed the negative principle of efficiency into an instrument for legislation and judicial policy-making. The 'Kaldor/Hicks test', as it is now formulated, holds that any reallocation of property rights is acceptable so long as it generates more gain to the winners than loss to the losers. This means that, in principle, the winners could compensate the losers and still have a gain left over. The emphasis here is on 'could compensate'; they need not actually make the transfer for the change to be efficient under the Kaldor/Hicks test.

To see how the Kaldor/Hicks test works in practice, let us return to our example of trading shoes for a television set. Suppose that the parties could not communicate with each other, but that some third party (call it the state) knew that party A wanted a TV set and that she was willing to pay five pairs of shoes as compensation. The third party also knew that B was willing to accept five pairs of shoes for a TV set. This means that under the Kaldor/Hicks test, the state would be engaging in an efficient move by taking the TV set from B and giving it to A. A could compensate B for the set and, under ideal economic conditions, she would simply have bought the set from B. But in our imaginary situation, the parties are unable to trade and therefore the state must do it for them.

The trick in the Kaldor/Hicks test is that each of the two sides to a transaction is analysed independently. That is, it is supposed that the transfer of the TV set to A is efficient whether A's five pair of shoes are given to B or not. In the original example of voluntary trading, the two transactions were conceptually linked—a TV set for shoes, and shoes for the TV set. The only basis we have for saying the trade made the parties better off is that they actually made the trade. Yet under the Kaldor/Hicks test of hypothetical trading, the single transaction splits into two. Moving the TV set from one party to the other is one move towards efficiency in the Kaldor/Hicks sense, and moving the shoes in the opposite direction is an independent move increasing efficiency.

Of course, you might be very puzzled by all this. You might think taking the TV set from one person and giving it to another, without actual compensation, is unfair. It violates the TV owner's rights to property. All this is true but it is of no interest to economists. Whether they believe in negative or positive efficiency, the free market and utilitarian economists agree on a common enemy. They are both clearly opposed to decisions based on the protection of rights—at least when rights are defined, as Dworkin defined them, as 'trumping' the social good. And they are both opposed to decisions based on fairness or justice, pure and simple. Of course, if rights, fair procedures, or just outcomes also contribute to the greater good, they are acceptable. The problem is when they do not. Perhaps the corn farmers in England had a right to hold on to their protective tariffs and their way of life that would be destroyed by free competition. No matter. If the collapse of these industries would have been good for the society as a whole, the economists would have rejected the right of the corn farmers to the status quo. If asked for a reason for this opposition, the economists might respond, as did Jeremy Bentham himself, 'Rights are nonsense, and natural rights are nonsense on stilts.'[5]

2. FROM NEGATIVE TO POSITIVE EFFICIENCY: ONCE MORE

The preceding tale of transformation is not nearly as dramatic as another story that began to unfold at the University of Chicago in the early 1960s. Since the late nineteenth century, the courts have occasionally relied on free market principles as a justification for liability in cases of 'externalities' typified by pollution and the other by-products of industrialisation. The basic claim has been that the law should serve to perfect the market by making each enterprise pay the full costs of production. Firms have to pay for the costs of capital and labour, but they do not have to pay for the social costs, such as sparks, air pollution, and noise, of the factories and machines they operate. According to the economic argument for liability, the free market cannot work properly unless

---

[5] J Bentham, *Anarchical Fallacies*, reprinted in *The Works of Jeremy **Bentham***, John Bowring (ed), (Edinburgh, W, Tait, 1843) vol 2 at 501.

these externalities are charged to the producers who generate them. Internalising the social costs by forcing the entrepreneur to pay for them leads to an efficient allocation of resources. The injuring firm's liability costs are subsequently passed on to consumers in the form of higher prices. Consumers make the ultimate decision of (negative) efficiency by purchasing those commodities that, in view of their costs of production and their harmful effects on others, best satisfy their preferences.

To see how this works in practice, think once more about the French ski slopes (generally a pleasant thought). If accidents on the slopes are an externality of running ski slopes as a business, then the price of a ticket should reflect the full social cost. If all sports internalised their accidents in the same way, then consumers who purchased participation in skiing rather than playing golf or sailing or power boating would choose through the market which sports they preferred, pleasure, health benefits, and accidents included. If the accident externalities are excluded from the price, the legal system indirectly subsidises the more dangerous sports.

The general principle is that 'Each industry (or sport) must pay its own way.' Lord Bramwell developed an argument of this sort in imposing liability against a railroad for emitting sparks and destroying an abutting farmer's crops.[6] Now associated with the name of the English economist Arthur C Pigou,[7] this principle has become the reigning view of externalities in the courts. It is an eminently sensible way of thinking about applying economic principles in legal analysis. The influential doctrine of 'enterprise liability' seems also to be based on the idea that each enterprise in society should bear the cost in human suffering it inflicts on the unwary. Because of 'the Pigovian principle' and its related doctrines in the law, we have witnessed an enormous expansion of product liability (that is, when products cause injuries to consumers) over the last half-century. The expansion has been so great that many politicians now claim that US business is now less competitive than foreign producers who are not subject to the same demanding rules of product liability.

---

[6] *Vaughan v Taff Vale Railway* (1860) 157 ER 1351 (Exch Ch).
[7] The first edition of Pigou's *The Economics of Welfare* (London, McMillan & Co, 1932) was published in 1920.

Until the 1960s, this was the only available theory of externalities. It seemed obvious that the way to internalise the social costs of industrial enterprises was to make them pay for the harm they caused. But just at the time that tort theory seemed to have discovered the right way to integrate economic thinking into the law, Ronald Coase, an economist at the University of Chicago, burst on the scene with his article 'The Problem of Social Cost'.[8] His basic claim is that what Pigou said 'ain't necessarily so'. Imposing liability against polluters and other injuring firms is not the only way to achieve efficiency in the allocation of resources.

Coase's basic strategy for countering Pigou was to shift the focus of economic analysis from decisions by consumers to potential decisions by victims. To take Coase's example, a rancher and a farmer live side by side. One produces beef, the other grain for the market. Their costs of production are included in the prices they charge for their products. Their problem is that the rancher's steers intrude upon the farmer's land and destroy his crops. Does economic efficiency require that the rancher pay for the harm? The obvious answer for Pigou was 'yes' in order to ensure that the price of beef reflected the full cost of production. Not holding the rancher liable would subsidise the price of beef; people would buy more of it, and eat more beef than they would if the market worked perfectly.

Coase changed the focus of the analysis by asking the specific question whether the farmer would have an incentive at the margin to add more steers to his land. Let us refer to this steer as the nth steer. And to make things simple, we will assume he has two steers and wants to add a third. Will the market encourage him to do this? Coase proved that whether he would do this or not was not a function of whether he was liable for the damage the third steer would do to the farmer's crops.

To make his case, Coase outlined four variations of the factual situation. In cases I and II, the steer can generate $300 in revenue for the rancher, and the crop damage is $200. In cases III and IV, the figures are reversed: $200 for the rancher and $300 damage to the farmer.

Case I: *Premises:* $300 gain for rancher; $200 loss for farmer. According to the law, the rancher is liable for the damage by the steer.

---

[8] (1960) 3 *Journal of Law and Economics* 1.

Consequence:	Rancher grazes the steer and pays farmer $200 in damage costs. He retains $100 of the gain.
Case II: *Premises:*	$300 gain for rancher; $200 loss for farmer. According to the law, the rancher is not liable for the damage.
Consequence:	The rancher will graze the third steer and not pay compensation to the farmer.
Case III: *Premises:*	$200 gain for rancher; $300 loss for farmer. According to the law, the rancher is liable for the damage.
Consequence:	Rancher will not graze the steer because his loss in liability costs to the farmer ($300) would be greater than the potential gain ($200) from the steer.
Case IV: *Premises:*	$200 gain for rancher; $300 loss for farmer. According to the law, the rancher is not liable for the damage.
Consequence:	Even though the rancher is not liable for the damage, negotiations between rancher and farmer will result in the steer's not grazing. It will be worth it to the farmer to offer the rancher more than $200 but less than $300 (the loss that would occur from grazing) to induce the rancher not to graze the steer, and it will be in the rancher's interest to accept some sum greater than $200 from the farmer in place of the $200 he could earn from grazing the steer.

The results can be summarised in the following table:

	Rancher liable for Crop Damage	Rancher not liable for Crop Damage
$300 rancher/$200 farmer	Case I: Result: Steer grazes, rancher pays $100.	Case II: Result: Steer grazes; rancher pays nothing
$200 rancher/$300 farmer	Case III Result: Steer does not graze; no money exchanged	Case IV Result: Steer does not graze; rancher pays between $300 and $200 to keep steer off land

This is all there is to the Coase theorem. In cases I and II, the steer grazes; in cases III and IV, it does not. This is a consequence not of liability but of the economic productivity of the rancher and the farmer. If it is worth it to the rancher and farmer to have the steer graze, it will graze; if not, it will not graze. It goes without saying that the same method applies to any conflict over whether a single resource, such as land or air, should be used in one way or another. You could play out the same argument in a dispute about smoking in restaurants or industrial pollution. The only assumptions necessary are that parties seek gain, that they are able to bargain with each other, and that they have full information about alternatives in the market.

The only move in this demonstration that might puzzle the non-economist is the resolution of case IV: the farmer will 'bribe' (as economists playfully say) the rancher not to graze the steer if the numbers so dictate. The rancher will accept the bribe and hold back the steer. It seems unfair that a potential victim should have to pay 'protection' to someone who might injure him. It is indeed unfair, but the premise of the economic argument is that fairness is irrelevant. It is efficient for the potential victim to pay not to be injured, and efficiency is the only value at stake.

Although this brief demonstration is sufficient to prove Coase's theorem, his classic article is devoted largely to a second attack on Pigou. It seems very important to Coase to undermine the judgments that courts routinely make about who causes what. The point of this attack is clear. Pigovian analysis presupposes that we can determine which enterprises cause which injuries, that we can carry out the task that Professor Guido Calabresi, one of the first lawyers working on law and economics, dubbed 'cost accounting'. That is, can we know that skiing accidents are an externality of running ski slopes? What if they are an externality of manufacturing skis or of the private decisions of the skiers to engage in the sport? A little scepticism enables us to perceive the victim as a causal factor in his or her own suffering. That is, the victim brings the externality to the ski slope, not the ski slope to the victim.

All the examples can be turned on their head. If the farmer insists on planting next to the railroad, then of course his crops will be destroyed by spark-induced fires. If pedestrians walk near the highway, then they participate in bringing on accidents with cars. If it takes two to tango, then, according to Coase, it also takes two to create pollution, an accident, or, indeed, any externality. The victim is as much of a cause as the industrial enterprise.

It is appropriate to refer to this way of thinking as 'causal nihilism'. We don't really know whether the fist or the nose causes the punch to the nose. Both are necessary factors. Although this causal nihilism is not a necessary part of the economic proof of Coase's theorem, it is a critical part of the general attack on the Pigovian tradition. The latter depends on intuitive causal judgments as to who causes what. We just assume that factories cause pollution, that dangerous activities entail accidents, that publishing newspapers generates defamation. The supporters of the Coase theorem call these intuitive relationships into questions, not because they must do so in order to prove their theorem, but they must do so in order to undermine the intuitive judgements that support the Pigovian theory of externalities.

In formulating alternatives to economic analysis of the law, the first line of defence must be the principle of causation. This was evident as early as 1973 in Richard Epstein's first article defending the principle of fairness in tort judgments: the paradigm he chose was a punch on the nose.[9] If the causal connection in a right hook to the face is not obvious, then nothing is obvious. Attitudes about causation, as it turns out, are more fundamental than generally assumed in shaping various approaches to tort liability. Either you take things as they are (a punch is a punch is a punch) or you insist that the world conform to your theory (a punch requires the meeting of two forces, a nose and a fist).[10]

The Coase theory, it should be remembered, is a theorem about the law's irrelevance. The rancher and the farmer will reach an efficient accommodation no matter what the law says. If that is the nature of the theorem, how could it become the most frequently cited article in the American literature? Lawyers generally do not pay attention to matters that are totally irrelevant to their practical tasks. The mystery, therefore, is how the Coase theorem underwent a metamorphosis from a critique of Pigou's theory into a tool for analysing liability in real cases of economic conflict.

---

[9] See Richard A. Epstein, 'A Theory of Strict Liability' (1973) 2 *Journal of Legal Studies* 151.

[10] For the distinction between these two modes of thought, see Bruce A Ackerman, Robert C Ellickson, and Carol M Rose, *Perspectivies on Property Law,* (Aspen, Law and Business Publications, 2002).

Coase's many enthusiasts found a technique for adapting his theorem to imperfect markets. The argument goes likes this:

1. Under ideal conditions, the market will produce efficient results.
2. Efficiency is good.
3. Where the market does not operate perfectly, where there is imperfect information or impediments to bargaining, the courts must intervene.
4. What should the courts do? They should allocate liability in an effort to generate the result that a free market would generate if it could operate. This requires a judgment about who would pay for what if they could.
5. Why should courts do this? Because efficiency is good. (See step 2 above.)

There we have it. A plausible defence for converting the Coase theorem into a standard for resolving concrete disputes: mimic the market by assigning rights and liabilities. This particular manipulation of economic ideas should not come as a surprise. It replicates the transition from negative to positive efficiency that led to collective intervention under the Kaldor/Hicks test. We express the same transition in these five steps. In step 2, efficiency is understood as the negative efficiency of free trade. The judgment about who would pay for what if they could (step 4) requires an interpersonal comparison of capacity to pay. In the end, we have the same principle of positive efficiency that grounds the Kaldor/Hicks test. This transition from negative efficiency to positive efficiency is too tempting to worry about logical consistency. It is necessary to convert the theory of the market into a standard that will support and justify judicial intervention to enable the market to reach an efficient result.

3. THE IMPLICATIONS OF COST–BENEFIT ANALYSIS

Economists would like to believe that the principle of positive efficiency is deeply rooted in the common law. They find it in the Learned Hand test for negligence, which imposes a four-part formula on the assessment of risk.[11] In order to decide whether a

---

[11] *United States v Carroll Towing Co*, 159 F.2d 169 (2d Cir, 1947).

risk is reasonable and justified, the finder of fact (judge or jury) assesses the possible consequences, good and bad, and the probably of each. Suppose the issue is driving a sick child to the hospital when the only means available is a car with defective brakes. The 'benefit (B) is calculated by imposing a value on the life and health of the child as modified by the probability that getting him to the hospital will incrementally increase his chances of survival. This is represented by P(B), the probability that the benefit will accrue as a result of using the defective car. The cost (C) is the potential damage that could occur to the child and to others in an accident on the way to the hospital. This factor is also modified by the probability of occurrence. Thus the question is whether P(B) is greater or less than D(C) whether the expected benefit is greater or loss than the expected cost.

The common law had always lent itself it to this kind of utilitarian analysis of risks with its seductive appearance of mathematical precision. The Continental tradition takes different approaches. The systems based on the *Code Civil* speak of the *bon père de famille* [good father of a family] as the exemplar of conduct showing due regard for the interests of others. The Germans simply defined due care as *die im Verkehr erforderliche Sorgfalt* [the amount of care or attention to risk required under the circumstance]. Neither of these Continental standards lends itself directly to cost–benefit analysis. It is understandable, then, with the utilitarian leanings of the Bentham school and the Learned Hand test already in place, that the economists would find fertile ground for the application of an economic theory of tort law—economic as understood in the Benthamite tradition.

The basic assumption behind the economic theory of negligence is that efficient defendants should be rewarded for their socially productive risk-taking and the socially inefficient should be punished by being required to pay for the consequent losses. This seems straightforward enough but the reality of tort law makes these decisions much more difficult. First, how can the economist properly take into consideration the plaintiff's behaviour, particularly contributory or comparative negligence?[12] Perhaps the cheapest the way to resolve the conflict in speeding motorist/pedestrian

---

[12] We address the problem of contributory and comparative negligence in ch 3, section 2 below in the analysis of *Nga Lee v Yellow Cab*.

accidents is to require pedestrians to use a flashlight when they go out walking at night. If they do not do so and they are injured, they will be presumed to be at least partially responsible for their own injuries. There are at least two parties who could take actions to minimise the social harm of their interaction, and it is not easy to figure how to coordinate their taking measures to minimise the harm in the long run. This has been a challenging problem for theorists committed to efficiency as the guiding standard of tort liability.[13]

The commitment to efficiency raises two problems of political theory which have not been properly addressed in the literature. The first is whether it is legitimate for a judge, serving in a national legal system, to seek the greatest good of all in his or her decisions in particular cases. To achieve a correct cost–benefit or utilitarian analysis, the judge must consider not only the interests of the parties in court but those of all the potential victims and risk-creators in the world (and in future generations) affected by the decision. The decision might be in the interest of Americans (say, American cigarette companies) and yet violate the interests of foreigners who become addicted to smoking as a result of aggressive cigarette advertising. Judges take an oath to uphold their local constitutions as well as to do justice. They take no oath to promote the public interest either at home or abroad. As a result, the idea that judges should promote world-wide efficiency seems at odds with their basic national commitments.

The second problem is why a judge of the common law or any legal system should be interested in promoting the efficiency of the court's decisions. It is not a very good answer that the court's decision to pursue efficiency would itself generate an efficient judicial system. The judge's decision might be interpreted by society in a way that generates overall inefficiency. Suppose that in a particular case it seems to a judge better to use the car with defective brakes than not to take the child to the hospital at all. He might rank the benefits as 60 and the burdens as 40. The public might understand this decision to mean that anytime there is a need to help a child,

[13] Tai-Yeong Chung, 'Efficiency of Comparative Negligence: A Game Theoretic Analysis' (1993) 22 *Journal of Legal Studies* 395, and Daniel L Rubinfeld, 'The Efficiency of Comparative Negligence' (1987) 16 *Journal of Legal Studies* 375.

it is all right to drive in violation of safety regulations. Given the way the decision might impact on society, the overall effect might be 60/80, or inefficient. There is no necessary correlation between the way judges see the case and the way the case will be interpreted by the public. Whether the impact is efficient or not ultimately depends on the case's impact on public behaviour, not on the judge's intention.[14] A decision may seem efficient on its facts, but it might turn out in practice to be inefficient. The opposite correlation might also be true.

An easy illustration of this conflict is that it might be better for judges to apply black-letter rules that everyone understands than to engage in the minute balancing of interests that the standard of negligence requires. There was a time, for example, when the courts adhered to a strict 'stop, look, and listen' rule for cars approaching railroads.[15] If the driver proceeded without stopping, looking, and listing for an oncoming train, he was treated as per se negligent. The courts abandoned this rule not because it was inefficient but it was considered unfair to use a single rule—one size fits all—to cover the huge variety of cases that might arise.[16] Judging the behaviour of the plaintiff and defendant 'under all the circumstances' might or might not be more efficient. Yet the argument of fairness seems straightforward: the general rule should give way to an evaluation of the particular circumstances of the accident.

To make things more complicated, there is no reason to assume that the fault standard is more efficient that the principle of strict liability for externalities, which, as Pigou taught us, internalises the externalities and makes the consumers of every risky activity pay the full price of that activity. Efficiency turns out to be a giant umbrella that houses a number of different theories that reveal both legal and economic diversity. When it comes to choosing among these theories, we should not forget what the parties to tort disputes themselves want to achieve. They obviously want to be treated fairly. If they have the choice between two systems of arbitration—one that would address the justice of their claims and one that would focus on the good of society—the normally

---

[14] See 'Paradoxes in Legal Thought' (1985) 85 *Columbia Law Review* 1263.
[15] *B&O Railroad v Goodman*, 275 US 66 (1927).
[16] *Pokara v Wabash Railway*, 292 US 98 (1934).

self-interested person (the economic person) would obviously prefer the system that focuses on the parties and their respective claims of justice. They seek justice for themselves—not the welfare of the unnamed millions who are not even aware of the particular dispute.

In the evolution of legal ideas in tort law—from trespass to fault, and back to strict liability—the guiding motivation has been corrective justice, that is, reversing the wrong that the defendant has caused the plaintiff by making the defendant pay for it. The sole exception might be the law of punitive damages, which seems to be heavily influenced by theories of deterrence and retributive justice—considerations more appropriate to criminal law. The ongoing influence of punitive damages in the tort system should remind us that the system of tort is a mixed bag. Economists have some impact, in some pockets of the law, but they surely do not rule. The claims of justice will be heard. Whether they prevail in the end depends on how rigorously and convincingly we can make the case for corrective justice in place of efficiency and other forces that drive the law.

3

Reciprocity

In the early 1970s the economists and the traditional tort theorists engaged in a pitched battle for the soul of the subject. For the economists, as outlined in the last chapter, the goal of tort law should be efficiency, in the particular case and for society as a whole. For the traditionalists, the purpose of tort law is to do corrective justice. The economists drew on everyone from Adam Smith to Coase. The traditionalists fell back on Aristotle, drew heavily on Kant's theory of deontological obligations, and found sustenance in Rawls' *Theory of Justice*, published in 1971. The heavy-hitters at the time were Richard Posner, Guido Calabresi, Richard Epstein, and, I suppose, myself—in light of a single article that seemed to state a coherent alternative to the theory of efficiency as the rationale of tort law.[1] The thesis of that early article was that the history of tort law was best represented as conflict between two paradigms of liability—reasonableness (or economic efficiency) and reciprocity. Articulating the theory of reciprocity drew many supporters because it provided a comprehensive and coherent alternative to the goal of efficiency in the economic approach to torts.

The paradigm of reciprocity has the capacity to systematise a vast body of rules governing tort disputes and to provide an alternative to the conventional analysis of tort history as tension between fault and strict liability. This conceptual framework of fault and strict liability accounts for a number of traditional beliefs about tort law history. One of these beliefs is that the ascendancy of fault in the mid- to late nineteenth century reflected, as Holmes argued, the infusion of moral sensibility into the law

---

[1] George P Fletcher, 'Fairness and Utility in Tort Theory' (1972) 85 *Harvard Law Review* 537.

of torts.[2] That new moral sensibility is expressed sometimes as the principle that wrongdoers ought to pay for their wrongs.[3] Another traditional view is that strict tort liability is the analogue of strict criminal liability, and that if the latter is suspect, so is the former.[4] The underlying assumption of both these tenets is that negligence and strict liability are antithetical rationales of liability. This assumed antithesis is readily invoked to explain the ebbs and flows of tort liability.

These beliefs about tort history are ubiquitously held, but to varying degrees they are all false or, at best, superficial. There has no doubt been a deep ideological struggle in the tort law of the last century and a half. But, in fact, the confrontation has been the paradigm of efficiency, on the one hand, and the paradigms of justice presented in this and the following chapter.

The paradigm of reciprocity shares a common feature with economic arguments: they are both based on the analysis and characterisation of risks. The economic argument is that liability is imposed for unacceptable risks and these risks are defined by what an unreasonable person would do under the circumstances. The terms unreasonable/unacceptable/wrongful run hand in hand with the principle of liability. The defendant is liable only if the risk is unreasonable and wrongful.

The paradigm of reciprocity concurs that risk-taking is the basis of liability, but the risks that can generate liability might be either reasonable or unreasonable, permissible or impermissible. The reason for imposing liability is not that the risk is inherently wrong but that it deprives the individual plaintiff of his or her due share of personal security. A good example is the case we discussed earlier of *Rylands v Fletcher*, where the builder of the reservoir was held liable for the flooding of his neighbour's land. The key to the case is the House of Lords' phrase 'non-natural use of the land'. For all its metaphysical pretensions, the phrase simply means the

---

[2] See Oliver Wendell Holmes, Jr, *The Common Law*, ed Mark Dewolfe Howe (Cambridge, MA, Harvard University Press, 1963, originally published 1881) [hereafter cited as *Common Law*] at 79–80; James Barr Ames, 'Law and Morals' (1908) 22 *Harvard Law Review* 97.

[3] See, eg, Lord Atkin's opinion in *Donoghue v Stevenson* [1932] AC 562.

[4] See J Salmond, *Law of Torts*, 6th edn (London, Sweet & Maxwell, 1924) at 12–13; cf Jeremiah Smith, 'Tort and Absolute Liability—Suggested Changes in Classification (Pts 1–3), (1917) 30 *Harvard Law Review* 241, 319, 409.

defendant intended to use his land for a purpose at odds with the use of land then prevailing in the community. He thereby subjected the neighbouring miners to a risk to which they were not accustomed and which they would not regard as a tolerable risk entailed by their way of life. The risk was non-reciprocal and it deprived the plaintiff, asymmetrically, of security. Even though there was no negligence on the part of the defendant, no fault, no immoral conduct, his imposing the risk on the defendant was a fair basis for liability. If everyone had reservoirs on their property, the analysis would be different. The risks would be reciprocal and therefore not an apt basis for liability. The Restatement of Torts has adopted this standard, much in the language it uses. The Restatement shuns the concepts of 'natural' and 'unnatural' and instead interprets the teachings of *Rylands* as imposing liability for an activity that is not a matter of 'common usage' and appropriate 'to the place where it is carried on'.

1. PRIVATE LAW, NOT PUBLIC LAW

The first principle in the paradigm of reciprocity, therefore, is that liability is imposed for the consequences of imposing a non-reciprocal risk on another person. The critical relationship is between the parties, not between the defendant and the public. Therefore, to pick up a theme that runs back to *Scott v Shepherd*, the question whether the risk is 'unlawful' is irrelevant. Concepts like unreasonable risk and unlawful behaviour focus on the relationship of the defendant to society as whole, not on the interactions of specific parties to the dispute. The focus of private law is precisely the relation of the risk to the welfare of the private parties.

By eliminating the element of unlawfulness, the paradigm of reciprocity also imposes liability without adverting to the defendant's duty. The basis of liability is not a breach of duty—there is no breach of this sort in *Rylands*.

The notion of fault is retained but in a limited sense. The defendant is not at fault in running the risk, but is nonetheless liable only if he or she is responsible for running the risk. Possible excuses, such as duress, insanity, and unavoidable mistake, are relevant in tort law as they are in criminal law. Thus, the second principle of reciprocity is that the defendant must be at fault in the limited sense of being responsible for imposing a non-reciprocal risk on the plaintiff.

The area that most consistently reveals the principle of liability for non-reciprocal risk-taking is the one that now most lacks doctrinal unity—namely, the disparate pockets of strict liability. Lawyers conventionally use this label to refer to cases ranging from crashing aeroplanes[5] to suffering cattle to graze on another's land.[6] Yet the law of torts has never recognised a general principle underlying these atomistic pockets of liability. The Restatement's standard of abnormally dangerous activities speaks only to a subclass of cases. In general, the diverse pockets of strict liability represent cases in which the risk is reasonable and justified under the paradigm of efficiency.

The typical cases of strict liability—crashing aeroplanes, damage done by wild animals,[7] and the more common cases of blasting, fumigating, and crop dusting[8]—clearly express the paradigm of reciprocity. If *Rylands* was one of the original cases in this line, the most discussed case today in the casebooks is *Boomer v Atlantic Cement.*[9] The defendant cement company was held liable in tort for polluting the air in the neighbourhood. This was a simple case of one side's depriving the other of a valuable asset. The notable feature of the case is that the court refused to enjoin the cement company from engaging in the polluting processes of production. Nothing could show more clearly that liability in this paradigm does not depend on the social disutility or the wrongfulness of the risk. Atlantic Cement was behaving lawfully and they could continue to pollute, but they had to pay for the harm done.

---

[5] *Ibid*.

[6] *McKee v Trisler*, 311 Ill 536, 143 NE 69 (1924).

[7] For example, *Collins v Otto*, 149 Colo 489, 369 P.2d 564 (1962) (coyote bite); *Filburn v People's Palace & Aquarium Co* (1890) 25 QBD 258 (escaped circus elephant).

[8] For example, *Exner v Sherman Power Construction Co*, 54 F.2d 510 (2d Cir, 1931) (storing explosives); *Western Geophysical Co of America v Mason*, 240 Ark. 767, 402 SW.2d 657 (1966) (blasting); *Luthringer v Moore*, 31 Cal 2d 489, 190 P.2d 1 (1948) (fumigating); *Young v Darter*, 363 P.2d 829 (Okla, 1961) (crop-dusting); *Smith v Carbide and Chems Corp* 507 F.3d 372 (2007) (potential strict liability from contamination caused by uranium enrichment).

[9] *Boomer v Atlantic Cement Co*, 26 NY2d 219, 257 NE2d 870, 309 NYS2d 312 (1970).

The paradigm of reciprocity also explains an old chestnut of tort law, *Vincent v Lake Erie Transportation Co*, a 1910 decision of the Minnesota Supreme Court.[10] The dispute arose from a ship captain keeping his vessel lashed to the plaintiff's dock during a two-day storm when it would have been unreasonable, indeed foolhardy, for him to set out to sea. The storm battered the ship against the dock, causing damages assessed at 500 dollars. The court affirmed a judgment for the plaintiff even though a prior case had recognised a ship captain's right to take shelter from a storm by mooring his vessel to another's dock, even without consent.[11] The court's opinion conceded that keeping the ship at dockside was justified and reasonable, yet it characterised the defendant's damaging the dock as 'prudently and advisedly [availing]' himself of the plaintiff's property. Because the incident impressed the court as an implicit transfer of wealth, the defendant was bound to rectify the transfer by compensating the dock owner for his loss.[12]

Without the factor of non-reciprocal risk-creation, all these cases—*Rylands*, *Boomer*, and *Vincent*—would come out differently. Suppose that Rylands had built his reservoir in textile country, where there were numerous mills, dams, and reservoirs, or suppose that two sailors secured their ships in rough weather to a single buoy. In these situations each party would subject the other to a risk, respectively, of inundation and abrasion. Where the risks are reciprocal among the relevant parties, neither party deprives the other of a valuable interest, such as security or clean air. A rule of liability does no more than substitute one form of risk for another—the risk of liability for the risk of personal loss. Accordingly, it would make little sense to extend strict liability to cases of reciprocal risk-taking, unless one reasoned that in the short run some individuals might suffer more than others and that these losses should be shifted to other members of the community.

---

[10] *Vincent v Lake Erie Transportation Company*, 124 NW 221 (Minn, 1910).

[11] See *Ploof v Putnam*, 81 Vt 471, 71 A 188 (1908) (defendant dock owner, whose servant unmoored the plaintiff's ship during a storm, held liable for the ensuing damage to the ship and passengers).

[12] Economists stress the element of contract in the case: see Calabresi, 'The Decision for Accidents: An Approach to Nonfault Allocation of Costs' (1968) 78 *Harvard Law Review* 713.

One fashionable argument for shifting losses in these cases resorts to the economic argument that some individuals have better access to insurance or are in a position (as are manufacturers) to invoke market mechanisms to distribute losses over a large class of individuals. This argument assumes that distributing a loss 'creates' utility by shifting units of the loss to those who may bear them with less disutility. The premise is the increasing marginal utility of cumulative losses, which is the inverse of the decreasing marginal utility of money—the premise that underlies progressive income taxation.[13] This is an argument of distributive rather than corrective justice, for it turns on the defendant's wealth and status, rather than his or her conduct. Using the tort system to redistribute negative wealth (accident losses) violates the premise of corrective justice, namely that liability should turn on what the defendant has done, rather than on who he or she is.[14] At stake is keeping the institution of taxation distinct from the institution of tort litigation.

The thesis, then, is that liability for non-reciprocal risk-taking provides a general account of strict liability. But this is just the beginning of the argument. Negligently and intentionally caused harms also lend themselves to analysis as non-reciprocal risks. As a general matter, principles of negligence liability apply in the context of activities like motoring and sporting ventures, in which the participants all normally create and expose themselves to the same order of risk. These are all pockets of reciprocal risk-taking. Sometimes the risks are grave, as among motorists; sometimes they are minimal, as among ballplayers. Whatever the magnitude of risk, each participant contributes as much to the community of risk as he or she suffers from exposure to other participants. To establish liability for harm resulting from these activities, one must show that the harm derives from a specific risk negligently engendered in the course of the activity. Yet a negligent risk, an 'unreasonable' risk, is but one that unduly exceeds the bounds of reciprocity. Thus, negligently created risks are non-reciprocal relative to the risks

---

[13] See Calabresi, 'Some Thoughts on Risk Distribution and the Law of Torts' (1961) 70 *Yale law Journal* 499 at 517–19; Blum and Kalven, 'The Uneasy Case for Progressive Taxation' (1952) 19 *University of Chicago Law Review* 417 at 455–79.
[14] See *The Nicomachean Ethics of Aristotle*, trs Ross (World's Classics edition, 1954), Book V, ch 4, at 114–15.

generated by the drivers and ballplayers who engage in the same activity in the customary way.

If a victim also creates a risk that unduly exceeds the reciprocal norm, we say that he is contributorily or comparatively negligent and deny recovery, in whole or in part. The paradigm of reciprocity accounts for the denial of recovery when the victim imposes excessive risks on the defendant, for the effect of contributory negligence is to render the risks again reciprocal, and the defendant's risk-taking does not subject the victim to a relative deprivation of security.

2. THE DISPUTE ABOUT CONTRIBUTORY AND COMPARATIVE NEGLIGENCE

Within the paradigm of reciprocity a controversy has raged for years about whether the proper standard of risk contribution on the plaintiff's side is contributory or comparative negligence. The story is worth telling in some detail, because the comparative dimensions are as rich as the domestic dispute about choosing the right standard. It is hard to believe but the French *Code Civil* of 1804 recognised no standard of fault at all on the plaintiff's side. The truth is that at the same date the common law did not have a standard for evaluating the plaintiff's contribution either. The first recognised common law case was *Butterfield v Forrester*,[15] in which the defendant put a bar across the highway and the plaintiff was riding without looking where he was going and tripped over the bar. The case sounds like one of the original examples on the difference between Trespass and Case, therefore it is odd that the reasons for denying recovery had not yet become conceptualised. The conceptual point of entry for a defence of contributory negligence was obviously the criterion of causation. If the plaintiff tripped over the bar, the defendant was not the primary cause of the accident.

The French also relied on the requirement of causation to introduce the principle that *faute commune* could bar recovery for negligence.[16] In 1900 the German BGB (Civil Code) section 254

---

[15] (1809) 103 ER 926 (KB).

[16] This proposition requires a question mark. The French sources do not discuss the plaintiff's fault, although the courts obviously consider the fault of the victim in practice.

formulated the first systematic approach to comparative fault: The contribution of each party was to be reduced according to its contribution to the resulting harm. The critical language was that liability would be reduced 'to the extent that the plaintiff's fault brought about the injury'. This principle of comparative causation became the now well-accepted doctrine of comparative negligence.

The dispute between the two ways of assessing the plaintiff's contribution to the reciprocal risk reached a high point of drama in a 1975 California case *Nga Li v Yellow Cab*. The case was a routine intersection collision in downtown Los Angeles. The trial court found that Ms Li had made a left-hand turn that was negligent under the circumstances and therefore she was barred from recovery. A reciprocal case of negligence on both sides undercut her case. The only way the plaintiff could win at the time was to shift the burden of risk to the defendant's side by alleging gross negligence or, more commonly, 'a last clear chance' to avoid the accident even after recognising the plaintiff's negligence.

Ms Li appealed on the ground that the state should follow the example of many other states and adopt the standard of comparative negligence, which would leave her the option of collecting at least a portion of the damages. Thus the court found itself in the middle of a major policy thicket. Could it adopt comparative negligence on its own, without legislative approval, and if so, which form would it adopt—the 'pure' form which would permit the plaintiff to recover a proportionate share of the total damages, no matter how great his fault, or the alternative system that imposes a cut-off when the plaintiff's fault exceeds 50 per cent?

The reasoning in the *Li v Yellow Cab* case was particularly interesting because the statute adopted by the California State Legislature in 1871 seemed to have adopted comparative negligence. Section 1714 in its original form read:

> Everyone is responsible, not only for the result of his willful acts, but also for an injury occasioned to another by his want of ordinary care or skill in the management of his property or person, *except so far as the latter* has, willfully or by want of ordinary care, brought the injury upon himself. [emphasis added]

The 'except so far as' clause seems directly to invoke the principle of comparative negligence. Nonetheless from 1871 to 1975 California adopted the 'none-or-all' standard of contributory negligence. Many Californian lawyers thought in 1975 that there was nothing to argue about, the original statute was clear, and that the standard of comparative negligence had prevailed all the time. But the Court could not accept the conclusion that it had been wrong for over a century. It affirmed the earlier rule, but then adopted its own version of comparative negligence beginning immediately. The only exception was for cases in which the trial had already begun under the old rule—they would still be governed by the traditional principle of contributory negligence.[17]

It turns out that the cleavage between strict liability and fault is not as important as the textbooks assume. Both strict liability and negligence express the rationale of liability for non-reciprocal risk-taking. The only difference is that reciprocity in strict liability cases is analysed relative to the background of innocuous risks in the community, while reciprocity in the types of negligence cases discussed above is measured against the background of risk generated in specific activities like motoring and sports. To clarify the kinship of negligence to strict liability, one should distinguish between two different levels of risk creation, each level associated with a defined community of risks. Keeping domestic pets is a reciprocal risk relative to the community as a whole; driving is a reciprocal risk relative to the community of those driving normally; and driving negligently might be reciprocal relative to the even narrower community of those driving negligently. The paradigm of reciprocity holds that in all communities of reciprocal risks, those who cause damage ought not to be held liable.[18] To complete our account of the paradigm of reciprocity, we should turn to one of its primary expressions: intentional torts, particularly the torts of battery and assault. Several features of the landlord's behaviour in *Carnes v Thompson*[19] in lunging at the plaintiff and her husband with a pair of pliers make it stand out from any of the risks that the plaintiff might then have been creating in return. An intentional

---

[17] This is an example of prospective overruling, quite common in constitutional cases, see *Linkletter v Walker* 381 US 618 (1965). (Note that the application of the exclusionary rule to state criminal actions (created in the Supreme Court case of *Mapp v Ohio*, 384 US 436 (1966)) was not applied retroactively).

[18] For a similar theory, see the theory of the 'risk pool' in Charles Fried, *An Anatomy of Values* (Cambridge, MA, Harvard University Press, 1970) at 177–93.

[19] 48 SW.2d 903 (Mo, 1932).

assault or battery represents a rapid acceleration of risk, directed at a specific victim.[20] These features readily distinguish the intentional blow from the background of risk. Perceiving intentional blows as a form of non-reciprocal risk helps us to understand why the defendant's malice or animosity towards the victim eventually became unnecessary to ground intentional torts.[21] The non-reciprocity of risk, and the deprivation of security it represents, render irrelevant the attitudes of the risk-creator.

It would be a mistake to think, however, that there are no important differences between intentional and negligent torts. We shall consider these in detail later in discussing the paradigm of aggression in the next chapter. It is worth noting now that the victim of an intentional tort is generally conceived as passive—as non-participating in the occurrence of the tort. In the case of an international tort, comparative negligence by the victim is irrelevant to the analysis. In its place there may be concern about assumption of the risk, a problem that we shall have to consider in due course.

The manifestations of the paradigm of reciprocity—strict liability, negligence, and intentional battery—express the same principle of fairness: all individuals in society have the right to roughly the same degree of protection against deprivation of their vital interest. Freedom from the risk of harm is properly considered one of these vital interests. By analogy with John Rawls' first principle of justice,[22] the principle might read: we all have the right to the maximum amount of security compatible with like security for everyone else. This means that we are subject to harm, without compensation, from background risks, but that no one may suffer harm from additional risks without recourse for damages against the risk-creator. Compensation is a surrogate for the individual's right to the same security as enjoyed by others. But the violation of the right to equal security does not mean that one should be able to enjoin the risk-creating activity or impose criminal penalties against the risk-creator. The interests of society may often

---

[20] For these purposes, 'intention' means knowledge to a substantial certainty that a contract will occur: see *Garratt v Dailey*, 46 Wash 2d 197, 279 P.2d 1091 (1955) (defendant, a young boy, pulled a chair out from the spot where the victim was about to sit down).

[21] See *Vosburg v Putney*, 80 Wis 523, 50 NW 403 (1891).

[22] J Rawls, *A Theory of Justice*, rev edn (Cambridge, MA, Harvard University Press, 1999).

require a disproportionate distribution of risk. Yet, according to the paradigm of reciprocity, the interests of the individual require us to grant compensation whenever this disproportionate distribution of risk injures someone subjected to more than his or her fair share of risk.

3. EXCUSING RISKS

If the victim's injury results from a non-reciprocal risk of harm, the paradigm of reciprocity tells us that the victim is entitled to compensation. Should not the defendant then be under a duty to pay? Not always. For the paradigm also holds that non-reciprocal risk creation may sometimes be excused, and we must inquire further into the fairness of requiring the defendant to render compensation. We must determine whether there may be factors in a particular situation which would excuse this defendant from paying compensation.

The difference between justifying and excusing conditions is most readily seen in the case of intentional conduct, particularly intentional crimes. Typical cases of justified intentional conduct are self-defence and the use of force to effect an arrest. These justificatory claims compare the benefits of acting with the cost of intrusion to the victim and come out, on balance, in favour of the permissibility of acting.[23] Assessing the reasonableness of risk-taking is the same inquiry but it is packaged as part of the definition of negligence rather than a distinct 'defence' called self-defence or necessity. The resolution of this cost–benefit analysis speaks to the legal permissibility and sometimes to the commendability of the act of using force under the circumstances. Excuses, in contrast, focus not on the costs and benefits of the act, but on the degree of the actor's choice in engaging in it. Insanity and duress are raised as excuses even to acts that are assumed to be unjustified and wrongful. To resolve a claim of insanity, we are led to inquire about the actor's personality, his capacities under stress, and the pressures under which he was acting. Finding that the actor is

---

[23] This is a simplification of the theory of self-defence: see George P Fletcher, *Rethinking Criminal Law* (Boston, Little Brown, 1978; Oxford, Oxford University Press, 2000) at 770 [hereafter cited as *Rethinking*].

excused by reason of insanity is not to say that the act was right or even permissible, but merely that the actor's freedom of choice was so impaired that he cannot be held accountable for his wrongful deed.

Excuses came into the law of torts by way of modifying liability of directly causing harm in trespass cases. One of the early discussions is dictum in the 1616 decision of *Weaver v Ward*,[24] where the King's Bench decided for liability but digressed to list some hypothetical examples where directly causing harm would be excused and therefore exempt from liability. One kind of excuse would be the defendant being physically compelled to act, as if someone took his hand and struck a third person. Another kind would be the defendant's accidentally causing harm, as when the plaintiff suddenly appeared in the path of his musket fire. The rationale for denying liability in these cases, as the court put it, is that the defendant acted 'utterly without ... fault'.[25]

If a man trespasses against another, why should it matter whether he acts with 'fault' or not? The King's Bench did not ask whether economic advantage would follow from holding that physical compulsion and unavoidable accident constitute good excuses. The question was rather: how should we perceive an act done under compulsion? Is it the same as no act at all? Or does it set the actor off from others? Thus, excusing is not an assessment of consequences, but a perception of moral equivalence. It is a judgement that an act causing harm ought to be treated as no act at all.

The hypothetical cases of *Weaver v Ward* correspond to the Aristotelian excusing categories of compulsion and unavoidable ignorance.[26] In *Rylands*, Judge Blackburn acknowledges these categories under the heading of '*vis major*' and 'act of God'.[27] *Vis major* corresponds to the excuse of physical compulsion recognised in *Weaver v Ward*, and acts of God are risks of which the defendant is presumably excusably ignorant.

---

[24] (1616) 80 ER 284 (KB).

[25] *Ibid*: '[T]herefore no man shall be excused of a trespass (for this is the nature of an excuse, and not of a justification, *prout ei bene licuit*) except it may be judged utterly without his fault.'

[26] *The Nicomachean Ethics of Aristotle*, above n 14, Book III, ch 1, at 48 ('Those things, then, are thought involuntary, which take place under compulsion or owing to ignorance').

[27] (1866) LR 1 Ex 265 at 279–80 (per Blackburn J).

Both of the Aristotelian categories have spawned a line of cases denying liability in situations of inordinate risk creation. The excuse of compulsion has found expression in the emergency doctrine, which excuses excessive risks created in cases in which the defendant is caught in an unexpected, personally dangerous situation.[28] In *Cordas v Peerless Transportation Co*,[29] for example, it was thought excusable for a cab driver to jump from his moving cab in order to escape from a threatening gunman on the running board. In view of the crowd of pedestrians nearby, the driver clearly took a risk that generated a net danger to human life. It was thus an unreasonable, excessive, and unjustified risk. Yet the overwhelmingly coercive circumstances meant that he, personally, was excused from having fled the moving cab.

An example of unavoidable ignorance excusing risk creation is *Smith v Lampe*,[30] in which the defendant honked his horn in an effort to warn a tug that seemed to be heading towards the shore in a dense fog. As it happened, the honking coincided with a signal that the tug captain expected that would assist him in making port. Accordingly, the captain steered his tug towards the honking rather than away from it. That the defendant did not know of the pre-arranged signal excused his contributing to the tug's going aground. On the facts of the case, the honking surely created an unreasonable risk of harm. If instantaneous injunctions were possible, one would no doubt wish to enjoin the honking as an excessive, illegal risk. Yet the defendant's ignorance of that risk was also excusable. Under the circumstances he could not fairly have been expected to inform himself of all possible interpretations of honking in a dense fog.

In these cases we have to ask: what can we fairly expect of the defendant under the circumstances? Can we ask of a man that he remain in a car with a gun pointed at him? Can we require that a man inform himself of all local customs before honking his horn? Thus the question of rationally singling out a party to bear

---

[28] See eg, *St Johnsbury Trucking Co v Rollins*, 145 Me 217, 74 A.2d 465 (1950); *Majure v Herrington*, 243 Miss 692, 139 So.2d 635 (1962). The excuse is not available if the defendant has created the emergency himself: see *Whicher v Phinney*, 124 F.2d 929 (1st Cir, 1942).

[29] 27 NYS.2d 198 (NY City Ct, 1941).

[30] 64 F.2d 201 (6th Cir), cert denied, 289 US 751 (1933).

liability becomes a question of what we can fairly demand of an individual under unusual circumstances. Assessing the excusability of ignorance or of yielding to compulsion can be an instrumentalist inquiry. As we increase or decrease our demands, we accordingly stimulate future behaviour. Thus, setting the level of excusability could function as a level of social control. Yet one can also think of excuses as expressions of compassion for human failings in times of stress—expressions that are thought proper regardless of the impact on other potential risk-creators.

These excuses—compulsion and unavoidable ignorance—are available in all cases in which the right to recovery springs from being subjected to a non-reciprocal risk of harm. We have already pointed out the applicability of these excuses in negligence cases like *Cordas* and *Smith v Lampe*. What is surprising is to find them applicable in cases of strict liability as well; strict liability is usually thought of as an area where courts are insensitive to questions of fairness to defendants. As we have noted in Blackburn's opinion in *Rylands*, however, the conventional Aristotelian categories of excuse are assumed to apply.

As a practical matter, the excuses of compulsion and unavoidable ignorance do not often arise in strict liability cases, for those who engage in activities like blasting, fumigating, and crop dusting typically do so voluntarily and with knowledge of the risks characteristic of the activity. Yet there have been cases in which strict liability for keeping a vicious dog was denied on the ground that the defendant did not know, and had no reason to know, that his pet was dangerous.[31] And doctrines of proximate cause provide a rubric for considering the excuse of unavoidable ignorance under another name.[32] In *Madsen v East Jordan Irrigation Co*,[33] for example, the defendant's blasting operations frightened the mother mink on the plaintiff's farm, causing them to kill 230 of their offspring. The Utah Supreme Court denied liability on the ground

---

[31] See *Fowler v Helck*, 278 Ky 361, 128 SW.2d 564 (1939).

[32] In *Fletcher v Rylands* (1866) LR 1 Ex 265 at 279–80, Blackburn J acknowledges the defences of *vis major* and act of God. Both of these sound in a theory of excuses. *Vis major* corresponds to the excuse of physical compulsion recognised in *Weaver v Ward* (1616) 80 ER 284 (KB), and acts of God are risks of which the defendant is presumably excusably ignorant.

[33] 101 Utah 552, 125 P.2d 794 (1942).

that the reaction of the mother mink 'was not within the realm of matters to be anticipated'.[34] This is precisely the factual judgment that would warrant saying that the company's ignorance of this possible result was excused, yet the rubric of proximate cause provided a doctrinally acceptable heading for dismissing the complaint.

It is hard to find a case of strict liability raising the issue of compulsion as an excuse. Yet if a pilot could flee a dangerous situation only by taking off in his plane, as the cab driver in *Cordas* escaped danger by leaping from his moving cab, would there be rational grounds for distinguishing damage caused by the aeroplane crash from damage caused by Cordas's cab? One would think not. Both are cases of non-reciprocal risk-taking, and both are cases in which unusual circumstances render it unfair to expect the defendant to avoid the risk he creates.

There is every reason to think that the principles of excusing risks apply across the board—in all cases of alleged tort liability. The recognition of this special category of issues remains, however, camouflaged in conventional tort doctrine. The reason is that the standard formula for defining negligence—falling below the standard of the reasonable person under the circumstances—applies in the paradigm of reasonableness both to assessing the risk and the responsibility for running it. By leaving juries to decide what a reasonable person would do under the circumstances, judges have found a way to collapse the two issues into one. Reasonable people, presumably, seek to maximise utility; therefore, to ask what a reasonable man would do is to inquire into the justifiability of the risk. If the risk-running might be excused, say by reason of the emergency doctrine or a particular defect like blindness or immaturity, the jury instruction might specify the excusing condition as one of the 'circumstances' under which the conduct of the reasonable man is to be assessed. If the court wished to include or exclude a teenage driver's immaturity as a possible excusing condition, it could define the relevant 'circumstances' accordingly. Because the 'reasonable person' test so adeptly encompasses issues of both justification and excuse, it is not surprising that the paradigm of reasonableness has led to the blurring of that distinction in tort theory.

---

[34] *Ibid* at 555, 125 P.2d at 795.

Beginning with Holmes' argument in 1881,[35] there has been considerable misunderstanding as to whether holding the parties to an 'objective' or 'community' standard of the reasonable person deviates from the standard of personal responsibility. The way to formulate this question correctly is to specify the issues that are supposedly suppressed by holding the parties to the norm of the reasonable person. One potential excuse clearly rejected is the claim of good faith. That fact that the defendant means well is hardly sufficient to excuse him for running an unreasonable risk. The leading case is *Vaughan v Menlove*,[36] in which a defendant was held liable for a fire that resulted from his keeping a flammable hayrick on his land. The defendant argued that he had acted 'bona fide to the best of his judgment' in maintaining the hayrick and in disregarding warnings that it was likely to ignite. But this could not conceivably be considered acceptable for endangering his neighbours. If it were, there would be no liability at all for negligent risk-taking. The cases left over, namely those in which the defendant knows of the risk and acts in bad faith to impose the risk on another, would be readily classified as intentional torts.

Confusion has resulted from *Vaughan* because the court also noted that the defendant did not possess 'the highest order of intelligence'. He was liable nonetheless. That stupidity is not an excuse should not surprise us either. Many criminals are of lower intelligence—particularly the ones who get caught. No one has ever got off a charge on the grounds that because he was less than bright, he was not responsible for his crime. Holding people to a community standard simply means that everyone must conform to the same standard of the law, even it is harder for some than for others.

The level of misunderstanding about these issues is overwhelming. Following Holmes, most writers in tort law assume that the 'objective' community standard implies a departure from the fault standard, but this is false. Negligence is based on the fault of not knowing and appreciating the risk.[37] In *Vaughan v Menlove*, the defendant was at fault for failing to listen to the advice of others

[35] *Common Law* at 107.
[36] (1837) 132 ER 490 (CP).
[37] See my article, George P Fletcher, 'The Fault of Not Knowing' (2002) 3 *Theoretical Issues in Law* 265.

when he should have known that his own judgment was likely to be flawed.[38]

It is true that judges sometimes use the '"objective standard' as a cover for disregarding certain excusing conditions in tort cases. The most notable example is the excuse of insanity, which is indispensable in the foundations of criminal liability yet readily disregarded in tort cases.[39] Another problematic excuse is teenage immaturity, which arguably should lead to verdicts favouring teenagers in cases of negligent driving that would not be tolerated if committed by adults.[40] Yet if courts disregard this potential excuse, their position could be justified by analogy to the objective standard in *Vaughan v Menlove*. It might be harder for teenagers to meet the adult standard, but that simply means that they must try harder.

There might be good reasons to deny excuses in tort disputes, even if the excuse were deemed an imperative requirement of justice in criminal cases. In tort disputes, there is an argument of justice on both sides. The plaintiff has a claim for compensation on the basis of an injury inflicted by the defendant. If the injury is inflicted unjustifiably, then the plaintiff has an even stronger case for recovery. Letting the defendant off the hook on grounds of a personal excuse creates a potential injustice to the plaintiff. This is particularly true in cases in which the plaintiff has relied on the appearance of normalcy. For example, drivers on highways assume that the drivers are competent, that they are not labouring under a condition—such as being teenagers—that will provide an excuse in the case of an accident.

This factor of reliance plays little role in criminal cases, but it is of great importance in torts. Those who visit medical specialists

---

[38] The theoretical differences between the subjective and objective standards of reasonableness as applied in cases of self-defence are explored at length in my book, *A Crime of Self-Defense: Bernhard Goetz and the Law on Trial* (New York, New York Free Press, 1988).

[39] *Ramey v Knorr*, 130 Wash App 672 (2005) (delusional driver still held liable for negligent traffic accident); *Williams v Kearbey*, 13 Kan App 2d 564 (teenager acquitted due to insanity in criminal trial still found to have committed intentional tort in civil trial).

[40] *Carter v Indianapolis Power*, 837 NE 2d 509 (Indiana Court of Appeals, 2005) (teenage driver driving at a high rate of speed 'jumping hills' was found to have committed contributory negligence relieving power company of responsibility due to poorly placed utility poles).

rely on the appearance of special training and experience. For example, the urban specialist cannot excuse his negligence on the ground that a country doctor would have done the same thing.

Yet there are cases in which the courts have emphasised the necessity of recognising the same excuses that would apply in a just system of criminal law. The doctrine of negligence per se holds that when the defendant violates a regulatory provision designed to protect particular categories of plaintiffs, the defendant should be held per se negligent. For example, if the defendant failed to provide fire escapes in violation of a municipal ordinance, the defendant would be liable if a fire claims victims who would have been saved had the defendant complied with the statute. These safety regulations often apply as a matter of strict liability in criminal cases—no excuses allowed. Yet the courts in tort cases apply a more sensitive standard and insist that only *unexcused* violations generate liability per se for negligence.[41]

These examples illustrate the difficulties of formulating a clear principle about the recognition of excuses in tort cases. The problem of justice to the plaintiff collides directly with the imperative of treating the defendant fairly. This is a deeper conflict than in criminal cases, where it assumed that the necessity of doing justice to the defendant prevails over the interests of both the state and the victim of the crime.

The question as to when excuses apply and when they do not is of critical importance in assessing tort liability for human rights abuses. States are typically involved in these violations, and when states are the primary actors, it is not clear whether excuses should be allowed. I have argued elsewhere that at the level of interstate actions, the criteria for excusing individual weakness in the face of danger should not apply.[42] This is particularly true with regard to claims of self-defence and reasonably mistaken self-defence. As collective actors, states cannot pretend to be subject to the same pressures of irrational behaviour as affect some individuals. This conflict must remain with us as we probe more deeply into the criteria bearing on ATCA liability.

[41] *Martin v Herzog*, 228 NY 164 (1920) at 168.
[42] George P Fletcher and Jens David Ohlin, *Defending Humanity: When Force is Justified and Why* (New York, Oxford University Press 2008) 125–8.

4. CRITIQUE OF RECIPROCITY

The principle of this chapter dictates liability for imposing non-reciprocal risks. Many economists regard the principle as too vague and impressionistic. After all, how do we know that driving an SUV is a non-reciprocal risk relative to riding a bicycle but reciprocal relative to driving a Smart two-seater? And where do motorcycles fit in? Are they more like cars or more like bicycles? This is all fair criticism, but there is just as much vagueness in trying to compute the factors that enter into assessing whether risks are reasonable or not. Whose interests count? How do we decide when risks are so unforeseeable that they are not included?

More to the point is a general critique of all arguments—both the paradigms of reasonableness and of reciprocity—for assuming that risks are identifiable phenomena in the world. Legal thinkers commonly assume that risks exist and are subject to assessment as objective probabilities. Supposedly it makes sense to say that if a specific individual drives with defective brakes, he or she is 70 per cent likely to cause a fatal accident within 48 hours. The problem with statements of this form is that they assume the ability to locate particular cases in classes of events.

Let me explain. Suppose we have actuarial tables showing that teenage drivers are more likely to cause accidents than adults. This may be true for the class, and therefore it is a reasonable basis for assessing insurance premiums, but this does not mean that we can infer a likelihood of harm in any particular case of teenage driving. Other factors must enter into the assessment—driving training, individual reaction time, coordination, and skill, not to mention the behaviour of other drivers on the road. Some factors—such as gender, race, and nationality—might be relevant but as a matter of policy we would not consider them. This leaves us with, at most, a very rough guess about probabilities in specific cases. As to any two drivers, one a teenager and one an adult, there is no way of knowing which of them is more likely to cause an accident.

This criticism is not likely to change the way lawyers think. Rational criticism rarely does. The entire doctrine of foreseeability in analysing proximate cause is arguably incoherent for the same reason that we do not know how to define the relevant class of events. The more abstractly the events in *Palsgraf* are stated, the easier it is to impose liability. Was there a foreseeable risk that pushing one passenger would result in injury to another? Of course there was. The more concretely the risk is stated, the more likely it is to appear unforeseeable. Was there a risk that touching a passenger carrying a package would cause a scale on the other side of the platform to fall on a mother from Brooklyn travelling with two children? Perhaps not.

If foreseeability remains the standard of legal analysis—despite its inherent ambiguity—there is no reason to think that lawyers will despair about correctly assessing the risk of harm associated with particular activities.

In a convincing critique of the paradigm of reciprocity, Jules Coleman pointed out an inconsistency with prevailing rules in the case law. In cases of contributory negligence, the critical question is not whether the plaintiff is engaging in a non-reciprocal risk but whether the plaintiff's negligence contributed causally to the harm.[43] If one person is driving with defective brakes and the other without lights, they are engaged in reciprocal risk-taking. But if the latter crashes into the former in such a way that good brakes could not have avoided the accident, then the fact of bad brakes is irrelevant to the case. Contributory and comparative negligence are based in fact on perceptions of comparative causation, not on comparative negligence in the abstract.

This seeming small point actually contains within it the entire critique of risk analysis in tort law. What counts in tort liability is not the ex ante risk but the ex post analysis of how the accident happened. Who caused what to whom? Both the paradigms of reasonableness and of reciprocity arguably place too much emphasis on ex ante risk analysis and are less than faithful to the rules that actually operate in tort cases.

Is there an alternative? In the next chapter I develop a paradigm of aggression that draws more on criminal and international law than on conventional thinking in tort law. As we shall see, this is precisely what we need to give a good account of tort liability for human rights abuses.

---

[43] Jules L Coleman, 'Legal Theory and Practice' (1995) 83 *Geo LJ* 2579 at 2609–17.

4

The Paradigm of Aggression

Human rights violations bear several characteristics that make it difficult to fit them into the paradigms of either efficiency or reciprocity. If we review the rights protected by the International Covenant on Civil and Political Rights (ICCPR), for example, we find persistent references to absolute rights, not to rights justified on grounds of their yielding a greater benefit than cost. It is true that, according to Article 4, many of the basic rights are subject to derogation in times of national emergency, and this suggests that the interests of state might prevail in some cases over the rights recognised by the treaty. But the possibility of derogation is severely limited. First, no derogation is permissible if it results in discrimination based on race, colour, sex, language, religion, or social origin. And, further, a whole list of provisions is exempt from the possibility of derogation even in times of national emergency. These include:

Article 6: The right to life, protected against the 'arbitrary' deprivation of life

Article 7: No torture, cruel, inhuman or degrading treatment

Article 8: No slavery or involuntary servitude

Article 11: No imprisonment for debt

Article 15: No liability for crime with prior recognition of the offence[1]

Article 18: Freedom of thought and religion, protected against presumably unreasonable interference.[2]

---

[1] This is not the precise statement recognised in the Latin formula *nulla poena sine lege* [no crime without prior legislative warning], because the provision acknowledges the possibility of offences recognised under international law, and we know since the Nuremberg trials that international courts do not always respect the principle of prior legislative warning. Cf European Convention on Human Rights, Art 7.

[2] Another provision, Art 16, is also non-derogable, but this does not make much sense. It provides that everyone is entitled to be recognised as a person. The pronoun 'everyone' already implies that the subject is a person.

These rights are violated by aggressive acts of the state—arbitrary killings, torture, degrading treatment, imposing slavery, imprisonment for debt, punishment without prior recognition of the offence, and imposing sanctions against the exercise of free speech. Except for setting the boundaries of free speech, the definition of these basic rights do not appear to admit of balancing interests. The rights are absolute. There is no conversation about the efficient use of targeted assassinations, or of torture, or of imprisonment for crimes made up on the spot. In the case of free speech and freedom of thought, in contrast, there is invariably a need to consider the harm that occurs by the exercise of free speech. Freedom of speech and freedom of the press are responsible for a host of harms—more than most people realise. Think of all the crimes committed by using language—everything from copyright violation, to counterfeiting, to forming conspiracies. In addition, hate speech can incite violence. Obscenity allegedly degrades women. No country in the world is as liberal about recognising freedom of speech and the press as is the United States, and even under the nearly sacred First Amendment there are many limits to harmful speech.

More important for our purposes, however, is the number of human rights norms that are cast as absolutes. In these situations, the state is the aggressor and the victim is the passive object of attack. These are the grave breaches of the Third Geneva Convention, which all states are treaty-bound to prohibit with their internal penal sanctions:[3]

(1) wilful killing, torture, or inhuman treatment [of any protected person], including biological experiments;
(2) wilfully causing great suffering or serious injury to body or health [of any protected person];
(3) compelling a prisoner of war to serve in the forces of the hostile power; or
(4) wilfully depriving a prisoner of war of the rights of fair and regular trial prescribed in that Convention.

Note the difference in structure. The rights inferred from the ICCPR do not presuppose wilful commission. Some basic prohibitions—like those against killing and causing great suffering—would not make sense unless the modifier of intentional killing were added. Others,

---

[3] Third Geneva Convention, Art 130.

most notably torture, have the required intention built into them. By comparison, all of the prohibitions in Common Article 3 of the Geneva Conventions are stated without a prior reference to culpability:

(a) violence to life and person, in particular murder of all kinds, mutilation, cruel treatment, and torture;
(b) the taking of hostages;
(c) outrages upon personal dignity, in particular, humiliating and degrading treatment;
(d) the passing of sentences and the carrying out of executions without previous judgment pronounced by a regularly con- stituted court affording all the judicial guarantees which are recognised as indispensable by civilised peoples.

Note that among these basic rights, some are subject to commis- sion by individuals—either soldiers or civilians—for example wilful killing, and again torture. Others require collective commission, most typically by the state, but perhaps by sub-state organisations. Note in this regard the offences that are connected to military operations, for example, the taking of hostages, compelling a pris- oner of war to serve in the forces of a hostile power. Compare those that imply the participation of something akin to a judicial system, namely those in part (d) of both lists.

All of these—plus additional provisions taken from the Hague Conventions and the Genocide Convention—have found their way into the Rome Statute of 1998, defining the crimes punishable by the International Criminal Court. This creates a wide range of international norms that could arguably be downloaded into the tort system applied under the ATCA. Whether there are limitations on the binding universal norms that can generate tort liability remains a topic that we must consider after reviewing the *Sosa* decision in chapter six.

The mode of thinking outlined in this chapter is appropriately called the 'paradigm of aggression'. The aggressor subordinates the passive victim to his will. The most common occurrence of this model is in the criminal law. As we shall see in the next chapter, the paradigms of the criminal law have had an enormous influence on the current understanding of the ATCA. Yet few people realise the cultural assumptions packed into the criminal law and the model of aggression. Therefore, we shall review these cultural assumptions in order to understand the way in which the model of aggression

can potentially shape litigation under the ATCA. The most significant of these assumptions is the concept of the victim as the passive
object of aggression.

1. THE PASSIVE VICTIM

In the criminal law we assume that victims are the bearers of
rights that permit them to expose themselves to risk. They are
entitled to move in the world with as much freedom as they enjoy
behind locked doors. They are entitled to walk in the park when
they please and to leave their windows open at night. A woman is
entitled to wear skimpy clothes without having to fear that she will
be faulted for precipitating rape. Bernhard Goetz is entitled to enter
a subway carriage and sit down among four rowdy black youths,
although everyone else in the carriage is grouped at the other end.[4]
This is what it means to be a free person, and the criminal law protects this freedom by not censuring those who expose themselves,
perhaps with less than due care, to risks of criminal aggression.
The blame is properly placed on the mugger, the thief, and the
rapist, regardless of the victim's role in the interaction leading to
the crime.

In criminal law, as opposed to tort law, there is no room to
argue 'assumption of risk'. It is no defence to rape to claim that the
woman assumed the risk by walking late at night in the park. The
notion of freedom implies that the victim who chooses to expose
herself to risk is to be treated in the same way as the victim at home
in bed. Admittedly, this way of thinking reflects our choice to view
the victim as a contributing factor or as a passive bearer of the right
to be left alone. The criminal law chooses the latter perspective
and that point of view that controls our thinking in analysing state
responsibility for violating basic human rights.

We may choose to remain in societies that inflict abuses on their
citizens. But there is no room in this context to argue that the
victims assume the risk of human rights abuses. In this the victims
who claim compensation under the ATCA draw on a deep tradition
of victimhood in Western culture.

---

[4] See George P Fletcher, *A Crime of Self-Defense: Bernhard Goetz and the Law
on Trial* (New York, New York Free Press, 1988).

In virtually all the languages of the biblical world, the notion of the *korban*, or *victima*, is linguistically tied to a certain form of temple sacrifice.[5] That is, the same word is used in court as in the temple. This is the pattern in Semitic as well as in Germanic, Romance, Slavic, and indeed all languages in the cultures of Abraham (that is Jews, Christian, and Muslims). To give a few examples, the term in Hebrew and Turkish is *korban*; in Arabic, *dchiyah*; in German, *Opfer*; in Polish, *offiera*; in Russian, *zhertva*. In Romance languages the term is a variation on victim or the Latin *victima*. The term *victima* is used throughout the Vulgate version, but in the English versions of the Bible, the word 'sacrifice' often takes its place. The important thesis is that the linguistic correlation is almost perfect. So far as I know there are no exceptions in any culture that reads the book of Leviticus.

In the original biblical context, the *korban* refers to the sacrifice made to cleanse the people of their sins and their guilt. The sacrificial animal had to be 'without blemish'—innocent—in order to bear the sins of the people. It is no accident that Jesus is referred to as the *korban*, the Pascal sacrifice to redeem the people for their sins.

The surprise, historically, is that the term has come to refer, as well, to the victim of crime. This second sense of *korban* does not appear in the Bible, but it pervades the language of everyone who reads the Bible—all Christian, Jews, and Muslims. The correlation between the two senses of victimhood is complete and astounding.

This linguistic correlation should stop us dead in our tracks. How is this possible? And what does the cunning of language tell us about the deeper meaning of victimhood in the criminal law?

The central idea of Leviticus is that the priests are able to transfer the guilt of the people to the sacrificial animal, the *korban*. Built into this scheme is the idea that the world is divided into two categories—the guilty and the innocent. Those who serve as the victims of sacrifice must be innocent, without blemish.

For good or for ill, we also make this assumption in contemporary criminal law and now in thinking about human rights abuses. There are the guilty and the innocent. It is hard to find a middle ground. This explains why if the victims of crime contribute to their fate by walking in the park late at night or associating with violent people

[5] See Leviticus 1:2.

or leaving their cars unlocked, we do not deduct their contributory fault or assumption of risk from the offender's guilt.

With a little sociological sophistication, however, we should realise that the sharp dichotomy between the guilty and the innocent purposely misrepresents the world of crime. Many, if not most, homicides and thefts are committed as the result of an interaction between offender and victim. Most murder victims are acquainted with those who kill them. Victims of fraud and embezzlement stand, by definition, in commercial interaction with those who misappropriate their assets. And, of course, date rape makes up a significant element of the statistics on rape. These are features of crime that presumably have been obvious for centuries.

Perhaps because it is so obvious that victims interrelate with their offenders, the criminal law exaggerates what we know to be false, or at least probably false—dividing the world into the distinct categories of the good and the bad. The dichotomy also functions to fend off suggestions that society is partially to blame for the offender's falling foul of the law. By cultivating the concepts of guilt and of victimhood, we can systematically camouflage the reality of criminal interactions.

2. INTERACTION AS THE ALTERNATIVE

As a whole, tort law has moved toward greater recognition of the interaction of victim and tortfeasor as the basis of liability. Thus we witness the triumph of comparative negligence in the common law, and the rise of apportionment among defendants as a way of allocating liability in shares to parties who have contributed more or less to the harm. The guiding principle of modern tort law is that each should pay according to his contribution. This principle extends so far as to impose liability on the basis of market shares for the marketing of birth control pills that, unexpectedly, cause cancer in the daughters of those who originally took the pills.[6] Everyone who participated in the market is liable on the assumption that market share correlates with the damage actually caused, even though the causal links between particular manufacturers and

---

[6] *Sindell v Abbot Laboratories*, 26 Cal 3d 588, 163 Cal Rptr 132 (1980), cert denied 101 US SCt 286 (1980).

victims can never be established. Of course, criminal law has also retreated more and more from imposing liability for harming specific victims by imposing more and more liability for the inchoate activities of attempts, conspiracy, possession, and risk creation without causing harm. Tort law, at least, insists on a particular victim. There must be real damage to someone before we even think about who might be liable in tort.

The intersection of criminal law and tort law in ATCA cases, therefore, represents a conservative approach to both fields. Tort law expresses the ties it once had to criminal sanctions. And the criminal law represented in this intersection is a throwback to the time when crimes were not merely an inchoate threat but claimed real victims.

There are two ways, then, to conceptualise the routine injury of A hitting B. According to the paradigm of aggression, A asserts himself by hitting a passive B and thus subjects B to his will. According to the model of failed interaction, it takes two for a hit to occur: both A and B contribute to the harm by failing collectively to avert the harmful contact. The critical difference is whether we perceive the victim as a responsible participant in the genesis of his own injury. That perception, in turn, depends on whether we see the two parties as engaged in a collaborative effort to minimise the harm latent in their interactions.

We can see the choice of perceptions in a case like *Brown v Kendall*. The defendant swings a stick in an effort to break up a fight between dogs. The plaintiff stands by. The dogs move around; the defendant and plaintiff move with them. Eventually the stick hits the plaintiff in the eye. We could focus narrowly on this interaction and see it just as an act of aggression and dominance. The defendant's swing injures the passive plaintiff; the stick encroaches upon his freedom. But we could also see the interaction as a collective failure of the parties to prevent the injury. The alternative paradigm of 'failed collaboration' holds the injurer and victim jointly responsible for the minimisation of harm. When the stick makes contact with the eye, either the bearer of the eye or the bearer of the stick might be seen as the causally dominant party.

The law and economics movement contributed to the rise of the model of collaboration by undermining our intuitive faith in unilateral causation. For Coase, a punch in the nose is no longer simply that. The nose is a party too. It did not have to be in the place where it would be hit. And the nose could have bargained with the fist not to strike. The possibility of these hypothetical bargains—the basic premise of the Coase theorem—creates a new vision of the world in which reciprocal causal phenomena are pervasive. In the world of potential deals there is no wrongdoer and no victim. There are only two people who have negotiated an efficient allocation of the right to hit someone in the nose. Tort law is no longer a wrong committed by A against B, but rather a failure of A and B together to collaborate and find a means to avoid accidents or at least to optimise their occurrence at point at which their joint costs do not outweigh their joint benefits.

Once you enter this world of interaction and collaboration, you see it all around you. The interactive dimension is expressed in the paradigm of reciprocity, which I presented in chapter three as an alternative to the theory of efficiency. In this context, at least, the notion of wrongdoing is maintained: the party that inflicts the non-reciprocal risk on the other is responsible for the damage.

By contrast, contract jurisprudence is the home not only of interactive parties but of the imperative of collaboration. The victim of a seller who does not perform is not entitled to play the role of the passive victim. If the market price is rising, thus giving the seller an incentive not to perform, the buyer can simply enjoy the seller's default and expect the seller to pay whatever it costs to procure the goods at a later date. The buyer bears a duty to mitigate damages by going out into the market and buying at the current price.[7]

This elementary doctrine of contract law expresses a distinctive way of conceptualising the relationship between injurer and victim. They are engaged in a collaborative scheme for their mutual welfare, and the breakdown of the scheme imposes burdens on the victim to minimise his losses. The victim of a contract breach bears no resemblance, then, to the victim of a mugging in Central Park. The duty to mitigate damages is characteristic of the paradigm of failed collaboration.

Yet, the basic principle of criminal law—the wrong of dominating another's physical well-being—survives and flourishes in the law of intentional torts, which is almost as indifferent to the victim's behaviour as is the criminal law. The primary difference between the two is that assumption of risk serves as a defence of varying

---

[7] See Uniform Commercial Code §2-712 (1978).

impact in tort cases, while in criminal cases of violent aggression, the victim's knowing—perhaps even voluntary—exposure to the risk is no defence. The same principle informs the pockets of strict liability in which we dispense with both the fault requirement and the relevance of the victim's contributory fault. In cases of abnormally dangerous activities, the defendant—when blasting, crop-dusting, fumigating, or flying an aeroplane overhead—directs a disproportionately great risk towards the plaintiff. The defendant dominates the plaintiff by imposing a non-reciprocal risk on him, but in the case of socially beneficial activities the law refuses to intervene prior to the realisation of damages. because the activity is socially beneficial; it cannot be enjoined as a nuisance, and the plaintiff may not interpose defensive force to protect his physical space. The subordinated plaintiff can do nothing except wait until he or she is injured.

My thesis is that the paradigm of aggression informs and shapes the law of liability under the ATCA. But we should keep our minds open to the alternative paradigms of tort law and their possible influence. In various ways the alternative paradigms are constantly encroaching upon the contours of ATCA liability. Whenever someone argues that perhaps torture should be justified in ticking bomb cases, the appeal is an indirect reference to the paradigm of efficiency. Ultimately the problem is whether we should be guided by the model of efficiency, the paradigm of reciprocity, or the paradigm of aggression. My thesis favouring the paradigm of aggression will become more plausible by engaging in a comparative analysis of two of the most important precedents, comparing *Filartiga*, which was the first case to establish liability under the ATCA for serious breaches of human rights, with *Sosa*, in which the Supreme Court upheld liability in principle for ATCA violations but denied liability in cases of unlawful arrest and short-term temporary detention.

5

Torture as Aggression

The great paradigm shift in the ATCA occurred in 1980 when the Paraguayan Filartiga family, whose son had been tortured and killed in Paraguay, discovered that the police chief of Paraguay, Americo Norberto Pena-Irala, was under administrative detention in the United States pending deportation. They believed that Pena-Irala was responsible for the crimes against their son, and they had medical evidence to prove it. They served process on him and thus began a suit under the ATCA as well as under several headings of liability. The trial judge dismissed the complaint for want of jurisdiction.

1. *FILARTIGA*: THE PIVOTAL DECISION

The Second Circuit reversed the decision, thus initiating the modern era of ATCA litigation.[1] Judge Irving Kaufman's opinion[2] for the three-judge court is a model of straightforward and passionate writing. First, he argued by reference to international treaties and expert opinion that official torture is a violation of the law of nations. Further, in order to counter some conservative case law about the state-to-state structure of international law, he reasoned that the law of nations applied to the relationship between a country and its citizens. The latter move did not seem to be a huge hurdle for, since World War II and the founding of the United

---

[1] *Filartiga v Pena-Irala*, 630 F.2d 876 (2d Cir, 1980) [hereafter cited as *Filartiga*].

[2] Judge Kaufman was famous for having sentenced Julius and Ethel Rosenberg to death after their conviction for espionage in 1952. He was said to have feared that he would be remembered primarily for that controversial decision. His decision in *Filartiga* generates a more nuanced picture of the man. See his obituary in the *New York Times*, 3 February 1992, p D10.

Nations, the trend of international law had been to protect resident individuals as well as foreign states.

Since the case was on an appeal from a motion to dismiss, the court did not have to cope with the contours of torture, whether the definition in the CAT was correct or whether the facts alleged in the case satisfied the criteria of torture. The court understood torture intuitively, as an evil, and they did not have worry about the borderline issues that trouble people today, for example whether certain forms of tough treatment like waterboarding constitute torture or not.

The more difficult problem for the court was whether the federal courts had jurisdiction over a suit brought by one Paraguayan against another about an incident in Paraguay. There were no points of contact with the United States except the service of process on the defendant. The US Constitution does not recognise diversity of jurisdiction of this type. The suit may be between citizens of different states, or an alien and the citizen of a state—but one alien against another was a pattern that the Constitution had not envisioned.[3]

Yet the court cleverly interpreted the law of nations to be part of federal law so that it could be said under the Constitution that an ATCA claim under the law of nations was one arising 'under this Constitution [or] the Laws of the United States'.[4] The steps in the reasoning are these:

1. International law is part of the common law.
2. The common law is part of federal law.
3. Therefore international law could be regard as part of the 'laws of the United States'.
4. Accordingly, a claim under international law was a claim arising under the laws of the United States.[5]

As we shall see in the next chapter, this syllogism came under severe attack after *Erie v Tompkins*, when the Supreme Court seemed to

---

[3] US Const Art III, § 2, cl 1. The provision that comes closest in Art III is § 2, cl 1, pt 9 ('The judicial power shall extend to all cases in Law and Equity between a State, or the Citizens thereof, and foreign States, Citizens or Subjects'). The first 'State' refers to one of the United States; the second to a foreign state.

[4] US Const Art III, § 2, cl 1, pts 1 and 2.

[5] For a historicist critique of this argument, see Curtis A Bradley, 'The Alien Tort Statute and Article III' (2002) 42 *Virginia Journal of International Law* 587 at 591.

change its position on proposition 2, namely whether the common law forms part of federal law.

This entire exercise, it turned out, served only to establish jurisdiction in the federal court. It did not imply that Filartiga's claim would be litigated under the law of nations. With jurisdiction established by the making of a colourable (that is, plausible) claim of a violation of international law, the attention of the Second Circuit shifted to the choice of substantive law, a decision left to the district court on grounds of 'fairness'. The court seemed to think Paraguayan law should apply as *lex loci delicti*. But this was not well thought out. The court knew little about Paraguayan law, not even whether torture was recognised there as a distinct tort. Also, the court did not seem to draw the proper inferences from the affidavit of the Paraguayan counsel, who said that some sort of civil recovery should be available but only after the perpetrator had been convicted of a crime.[6] There were no indications that the police chief might be convicted, and indeed it appears that another person had already been convicted of the torture and killing of the Filartiga boy. The prospects of civil recovery under Paraguayan law were in fact highly unlikely. This single example illustrates how important it is that we know more about the history and comparative analysis of torture before settling upon a regime for recovery for torture under the ATCA.

2. THE ODDITIES OF TORTURE

In *Filartiga*, the Second Circuit treated torture as self-evident evil, a violation of international law, and took it for granted that torture would be a violation of the local law and provide a basis for recovery. Had they investigated the details of Paraguayan law, they might have encountered a surprising lacuna in the law.

Torture as such was never recognised, historically, as either a distinct crime or a distinct tort. This is true of civil law as well as the common law traditions. You will not find the term in the French, German, or other European criminal codes. It is prohibited as a crime today under 18 USC section 2340 in conformity with

---

[6] See the Gorostiaga affidavit, quoted in the *Filartiga* opinion at 880.

the international Convention against Torture (CAT)—adopted internationally on the basis of a General Assembly Resolution of December 1975.[7] But this statute, oddly, applies only to torture committed abroad. This is subtle testimony to the concept's being foreign to US law. Other legal systems have equal difficulty absorbing the international ban against official torture. In a recent German *cause célèbre* about a police officer threatening torture in order to locate a kidnapped child, the public apparently thought it sufficient to label the offence one of 'coercion'.[8]

How do we explain the absence of torture from the traditional catalogue of prohibited actions? Is it enough to say that the crime and tort are covered by the law of battery? Murder and mayhem are also aggravated forms of battery but there is still a point to capturing the evil of each in a distinctive offence. If torture is a particular kind of evil action, then we should have expected a crime by that name to have coalesced in the history of the law. We can only be puzzled by the absence of the sources.

The ancient history of the concept is no more illuminating. With torture the primary theme in the execution of Jesus, one would expect to find the Bible overflowing with references to the concept. It is not to be found in the standard Gospel accounts of the crucifixion and, so far as I can tell, there is no prohibition of torture either in the New or the Old Testaments. To the contrary, one of the parables of Matthew pictures God as '[torturing] every one of you if you do not forgive your brother or sister from your heart'.[9] (I cannot attest whether this is a correct rendering of the Greek.)

In biblical Hebrew the term closest to torture is *'inui'*. The same term is used by the Israeli Supreme Court in its famous decision of 1999 prohibiting the use of torture in the interrogation of terrorist

---

[7] See Declaration on the Protection of All Persons from Being Subjected to Torture and Other Cruel, Inhuman or Degrading Treatment or Punishment, GA Res 3452, UN Doc A/10034 (9 December 1975).

[8] The police official in the case, Daschner, was charged and convicted of instructing a subordinate to commit an offence, while his subordinate was charged with coercion (*Nötigung*): Landgericht (District Court) Frankfurt, judgment of 20 December 2004, reprinted in *Neue Juristische Wochenschrift* (2005) at 692–6. The suspect under interrogation admitted, after being threatened with torture, that he had killed the boy. Although Daschner was convicted, the court invoked StGB § 59 and declined to punish him.

[9] Matthew 18:35.

suspects.[10] The term appears for the first time in the Bible in Genesis 34:2 to describe the crime that Schechem commits against Dinah, the daughter of Jacob, thus invoking the wrath of her brothers. This is correctly translated as 'humbling' or 'humiliating' Dinah— presumably an offence to her sexual honour. After wreaking destruction on Schechem and his people, the brothers justify their conduct by saying that Schechem had treated their sister as a whore.[11] Thus the term *inui* bears some relationship to torture but it would be incorrect to translate the crime as 'torturing' Dinah, although the New Revised Standard Version of the Bible comes close by rendering the offence as lying 'with her by force'.[12]

In the history of criminal procedure, the primary emphasis on torture was its positive benefit in eliciting confessions. The Continental system of legal proofs—based, by the way, on the biblical model—required some objective criteria of proof, a certain of number of witness, with certain qualifications. For example, women could not be witnesses; there was a difference in weight between the testimony of a nobleman and that of a commoner. This was the system of 'legal proof'. The indirect consequence was to confer a premium on the only acceptable alternative to the established mode of proof, namely proving guilt by confession. We see traces of this system in the constitutional provision requiring a conviction to be based on two witnesses to the overt act of treason or 'on confession in open court'.[13] Arthur Miller's 'The Crucible' provides a vivid portrayal of officials using torture in colonial Massachusetts for the supposedly necessary end of getting suspects to confess to their being possessed by the devil. Torture was considered evil, but an evil tolerated as necessary in many historical contexts, the primary value being to secure a conviction in the absence of the prescribed mode of legal proof.

The US Constitution takes a nuanced position on the problem. The use of torture in punishment is implicitly forbidden by the Eighth Amendment's ban on 'cruel and unusual punishments'.

---

[10] See HCJ 5100/94, *Public Committee Against Torture et al v State of Israel et al*, Supreme Court of Israel, judgment of 6 September 1999.

[11] Genesis 34:31.

[12] The King James Version reads 'defile her', also suggesting an offence closer to rape: see Genesis 34:2.

[13] US Const Art III, § 3, cl 1 (sentence 2).

Yet even though torture bears a close historical relationship to the securing of confessions, the Constitution permits, as we have noted, the use of confessions to prove treason, provided the confessions are made in 'open court'. The clause seems to assume that confessions taken in private might well be influenced by impermissible methods. But these methods—ranging from coercion to torture—are nowhere mentioned in the Bill of Rights. It took many decades of due process litigation to develop a refined law of permissible police interrogation.[14]

This is not to say that police torture for purposes other than securing a confession would be permissible. But the general ban on police brutality required other subtle constitutional moves, such as the application of the Fourth Amendment on search and seizure to cover the use of excessive force.[15] In both of these developments, the banning of torture was the by-product of setting higher goals regulating the conduct of the police. Eliminating torture—except in the case of cruel punishments—was never a constitutional end in itself.

Outside the realm of police and official state action, we run into other problems capturing the particular evil of torture. The law of battery covers most forms of torture but it would not include the subtle forms of humiliation covered by the biblical concept of *inui*. Thus battery and torture are intersecting sets. There are some cases of battery that are not torture, and some cases of torture that are not battery.

If we need a quick guess about why our attitudes towards torture have changed, I would say that our turning away from torture tracks our attitudes towards human dignity as an ultimate value. Today we are committed to protecting human dignity, and we see torture as a violation of that dignity. But the celebration of human dignity is a recent phenomenon, more recent even than the Constitution of 1789, which could engage in a wholesale violation of human dignity by institutionalising the ownership of human beings. It is not surprising that, in the wake of the Civil War, we should enshrine the equality of all persons born in the United States, and in the aftermath

---

[14] The process culminated in *Miranda v Arizona*, 384 US 436 (1966) (confessions cannot be introduced at trial when police have violated procedures required by the Fifth Amendment).

[15] See *Powell v Gardner*, 891 F2d 1039 (2d Cir, 1989).

of the Holocaust, that Germans should discover *Menschenwürde* human dignity as their basic constitutional principle.[16] Both the American commitment to equality and the German conception of *Menschenwürde* draw, I think it is fair to say, on the same conception of human beings made in the image of God.[17]

3. TORTURE IN THE CONTEXT OF ARMED CONFLICT

Prior to the nineteenth century, torture was not considered a prominent issue in the discussions of just war theory and the law of war. The modern discussion of the issue begins in Francis Lieber's famous code called General Order No 100 for the Union Army. The topic is raised, indirectly, in the following paragraph explaining the limits on military necessity:

> Art 16. Military necessity does not admit of cruelty—that is, the infliction of suffering for the sake of suffering or for revenge, nor of maiming or wounding except in fight, *nor of torture to extort confessions*. It does not admit of the use of poison in any way, nor of the wanton devastation of a district. It admits of deception, but disclaims acts of perfidy; and, in general, military necessity does not include any act of hostility which makes the return to peace unnecessarily difficult. (emphasis added)

This dense paragraph reveals a number of critical propositions about the law of war:

1. Military necessity does not justify everything. There are some absolutes that cannot be overridden by claims of necessity. The best example is the use of poison.
2. The ban on deception must admit of exceptions, therefore we have the subtle distinction between ordinary deception and perfidy.
3. Finally, we encounter a prohibition against torture, but curiously only for the purpose of extorting confessions.

Why should only this use of torture be prohibited? The answer might be that it distorts the process of proving guilt. It resembles

---

[16] *Grundgesetz* Art 1.
[17] This argument is developed in my article, 'In God's Image: The Religious Imperative of Equality under Law' (1999) 99 *Columbia Law Review* 1608.

the ban against coerced confessions developed in the jurisprudence on the Bill of Rights—and indeed around the civilised world—in the twentieth century.[18] But torture today has many aims other than securing a confession. It may be purely sadistic or designed to humiliate detainees, as in the Abu Ghraib prison, as a way of breaking their will and making them more submissive. It may be designed to secure the names and plans of other members of a military unit. Do the diverse purposes of torture matter? There are many oddities surrounding the concept of torture but one of the greatest appears in the Torture Victim Protection Act, enacted in 1991, to give the benefits of the *Filartiga* decision to US citizens as well as to foreigners. The statute contains the same curious style of definition that we find both in the Convention Against Torture and in the Lieber Code. The ban on torture is limited to 'severe pain or suffering' inflicted for one of three characteristic purposes. They are, essentially: obtaining a confession, punishing for suspected offences, and intimidation or coercion 'based on discrimination of any kind'. The implication is that torture simply for its own sake—to express the sadistic purposes of the torturer—would not be covered. In other words, it is not the action per se that is evil but the purposes for which it is used.

The CAT mentions the same three purposes, formulated more or less in the same way. No one pays much attention to these purposes in thinking about the permissibility of torture. The federal definition of torture drops the three characteristic purposes and concentrates exclusively on the type of pain inflicted. The key words are 'specifically intended to inflict severe physical or mental pain or suffering'.

The preoccupation with pain reveals a surprising indifference to the actual concept of torture as it used in our moral life—and particularly to the element of humiliation as we have seen it elaborated in the parallel biblical concept. We have a strong moral reaction to the practice for reasons that go much deeper than the infliction of pain or the various purposes for which it might be used. The problem with the torture memoranda written by John Yoo and Jay Bybee is that they take the intentional infliction of serious pain

---

[18] See, eg, *Weeks v United States*, 232 US 383 (1914) (federal courts must exclude ill-obtained confessions); *Mapp v Ohio*, 367 US 643 (1961) (federal constitution requires that state courts exclude from trial unlawfully obtained evidence).

as the only relevant variable in deciding whether mistreatment of persons in custody constitutes torture.[19] My view on their error is that they are less at fault than is the legal profession, which has tolerated, without critical objection, the oversimplified emphasis on pain in the international and federal definitions of torture.

4. AN AFFIRMATIVE ACCOUNT OF TORTURE

Anyone sensitive to ordinary language philosophy would grasp the disconnection between the federal focus on the intentional infliction of pain and the ordinary understanding of the concept of torture. Yet a full account of the concept has never been offered in the literature. As a first approximation of the concept, I would suggest three components:

A. *The relationship between the torturer and the victim.* This is typically a relationship of domination. The victim is totally under the control of the torturer. This is typically expressed in a binding of the limbs and an exposure of the body to the actions of the torturer. For this reason, harming an aggressor in self-defence—say, by biting his hand to the bone if necessary to avert the attack—is not torture, even if the same conduct in another context might be considered torture.

B. *The reflexive component.* The torturer not only knows that his actions have painful or otherwise intrusive consequences for the victim, but the torturer typically enjoys the infliction of harm. That is, there is a reflexive component in the continuation of the mistreatment. There is the first moment of pain or humiliation. The torturer recognises this and decides to continue the action, either as end in itself or for one of the purposes mentioned in the various statutory formulations. This reflexive component is appropriately described as enjoyment or at least as satisfaction. Sadism and torture are not coextensive but their relationship is complicated and needs to be sorted out.

---

[19] Memorandum from Office of the Assistant Attorney General to Alberto R Gonzales, Counsel to the President (1 August 2002) [the Bybee Memorandum]; Memorandum from John Yoo, Deputy Assistant Attorney General, and Robert J Delahunty, Special Counsel, to William J Haynes II, General Counsel, Department of Defense (9 January 2002) [the Yoo Memorandum].

C. *A sexual or prurient component—in many cases.* This appears both in inflicting the torture and in the public's fascination with the phenomenon. This was evident in the techniques of humiliation used against the Muslim detainees in Abu Ghraib. The use of female soldiers in the routines had obvious sexual overtones. The lascivious interest of the public is more complicated. The attitude is not only one of disgust (as it might be if the victims were forced to eat their vomit) but disgust coupled with intense curiosity and a desire to see the photos once again. A reflection of this prurient interest is found in the popularity of torture museums in various European cities. Of course, the curiosity is masked by outrage and the vow to prosecute the evildoers.

The Abu Ghraib incidents offer good counter-examples to any definition centred on the intentional infliction of pain. Most people would identify the technique of humiliation used in Abu Ghraib as torture, and once again it is good to be reminded of the biblical definition. The federal statutory definition includes 'mental pain', but no one has a clear idea what that is, that is, whether it includes humiliation or not. Of course, the natural tendency would be to make the federal and international definitions work by squeezing every recognised form of torture into the words used in the definition.

But Yoo and Bybee worked the other way around. They abandoned their intuitions for the sake of a literal interpretation of the legislative definition. Then they did a Lexis search for the words used in the definition and found an association in a totally unrelated statute between 'severe pain' and organ failure. Thus they concluded that organ failure provided a good threshold for defining when severe pain reaches the level of torture. I am not sure which was the biggest mistake they made. Most people are outraged by their reasoning by association about the meaning of severe pain in another statutory context, but I think the most serious error is taking the language of the statute seriously in the first place. In a recent book, Jack Goldsmith, Yoo's successor in the Office of Legal Counsel, criticised Yoo's literalism as inaccurate under the law, although he has little to offer by way of a better account of torture.[20]

---

[20] See Jack Goldsmith, *The Terror Presidency* (New York, WW Norton, 2007) at 145–51.

The best account I have seen of the legal aspects of torture appears in the judgment of Aaron Barak, then President of the Israeli Supreme Court, in which he outlines the means of interrogation permissible under Israeli law. Barak begins with the correct question: what is the nature of interrogation and what should be allowed, as a matter of administrative law, in the official questioning of prisoners? The problem is not who should be punished for inflicting torture but rather whether various techniques of interrogation should be declared, ex ante, permissible or impermissible.[21]

As we have noted, the US domestic solution to the problem has followed this pattern of regulating police behaviour. The US case law has never addressed the problem of torture in interrogation per se but rather assayed the larger question of how the police should be able to interact with suspects and use the evidence obtained to secure a conviction at trial.

For purposes of international law, however, the right question is not what is permissible police activity under domestic law but rather what is wrong under the shared standards of the international community. The models of criminal and tort law are better suited to a regime in which the domestic authority of local officials is of secondary relevance. Thus for purposes of the ATCA, we do not inquire about administrative authorisation but about the end result—what is wrong, tortious, evil, and what are the acts that require a response in the form of retributive justice.

5. THE ELEMENT OF STATE ACTION

In offering an affirmative account of torture, the element of state action is strikingly unnecessary. So long as there is a relationship of domination between the torturer and the victim, it is not clear why the official status of the torturer should matter. According to the CAT and *Filartiga*, however, only official state torture constitutes a violation of international law. Yet there is no reason to define torture under the domestic system of criminal law as an offence that includes an element of state action. We noted that, in the

[21] Judgment on the Interrogation Methods applied by the GSS (*Public Committee Against Torture v Israel*), HCJ 5100/94 (1999).

absence of a tort or crime called torture, battery would be a rough equivalent, though of lesser gravity. Battery, of course, is a crime or tort, regardless of the official status of the offender. But there could be a logical gap between the theory of jurisdiction used in *Filartiga* and the criteria of liability based on the domestic offence of battery. *Filartiga* relied heavily on a state-centred conception of international law with the modification that states may be liable to their own citizens for a violation of the law of nations.

But since 1980 our understanding of international law has changed dramatically. The law of the twenty-first century recognises the actions of individuals towards other individuals as elements of international law. This is true of the Rome Statute establishing the International Criminal Court, as it was under the International Criminal Tribunal for the former Yugoslavia and the equivalent international tribunal for Rwanda. More dramatically, the Supreme Court has endorsed individual liability under international law in its definitive interpretation of the ATCA in *Sosa v Alvarez-Machain*, decided in 2004.[22] In a very thoughtful review of the treatment of international law in Blackstone's *Commentaries*, Justice Souter concludes for a unanimous court that international law consists of three distinctive forms of liability. First, there is the traditional Westphalian principle of state-to-state liability. Second, there is a realm of international commerce—typified by the transactions regulated by the law of merchants—where individuals encounter trading partners under an international legal regime.

Finally, there is a system of individual liability in which the defendant's liability carries implications for the international system as a whole. The leading examples offered by Blackstone are common law criminal liability for piracy, for offences against ambassadors, and for violations of safe conduct. The Court adopts these three examples of liability as paradigmatic examples of what the ATCA meant, as read against the ambient law[23]—namely the common law as expressed in Blackstone's *Commentaries*—of 1789. The significant feature of all three is that they are committed by individuals—but under circumstances where the absence of relief could generate

---

[22] 542 US 692 (2004).

[23] It appears that the Supreme Court coined the expression 'ambient law' in *Sosa* at 714. It appears nowhere else in the entire Lexis data bank. About 12 law review articles refer to the term, just about all concerning *Sosa*.

international consequences. The purpose of the ATCA is to keep the peace by providing a quick and efficient remedy for the aggrieved plaintiff—the foreign victim of piracy, the offended ambassador, or the alien merchant whose safe conduct on foreign territory is impeded. Under these accepted examples of liability under the ATCA, the victim of privately enforced torture would seem to be an equally likely candidate for relief. Suppose that a foreigner named Haq is tortured by a private company called Greenwater that detains and interrogates suspects in Iraq. After he is released, Haq sues Greenwater under the ATCA by serving process on its representatives in Delaware. Torture is torture whether inflicted by a private company or a state agency. The current approach of the Supreme Court should support this interpretation.

The difficulty with insisting on an element of state action (say, by tracing Greenwater to the governmental agency that contracted its services) is that state action, particularly by the US government, invites a claim of sovereign immunity under the Foreign Torts Claims Act.[24] This was another contribution of the *Sosa* case in 2004: The US government is not in general liable for torts that occur abroad. But this is a very complicated subject beyond the scope of our present inquiry about the nature of torture. The important point is that torture inflicted by private parties could well be considered a violation of the law of nations. And even if the government and its officials are not liable under the ATCA, those who supply them with services and otherwise assist in their violations are liable, in tort, as accomplices for violations for the law of nations.[25]

6. *KARADŽIĆ* COMPLETES THE CYCLE

Fifteen years after the decision in *Filartiga*, the Second Circuit drew the proper inferences from *Filartiga* and established the liability of the Bosnian Serb Radovan Karadžić, in his personal capacity, for committing genocide, war crimes, and crimes against humanity

---

[24] 28 USC § 2680.
[25] For a good example, see *Almog v Arab Bank*, 471 F Supp 2d 257 (EDNY, 2007) (denying bank's motion to dismiss ATCA suit that alleged accomplice liability for knowingly providing banking services to terrorist organisations, in violation of the law of nations).

against the Bosnian and Croat population, Karadžić aspired to the leader of nascent nation but he had not reached that position and therefore had to be considered, for most purposes, as a defendant acting individually, not as the representative of an established regime. The District Court dismissed the charges against him for these reasons. The Second Circuit reversed and added another a critical cornerstone to the modern law of ATCA liability.

The Second Circuit, Judge Newman writing for the panel, unequivocally accepted an evolving conception of international law. It endorsed the findings of *Filartiga* and was willing to go further in updating international law to include the offences generated by the post-war tribunals in Nuremberg, the Geneva Conventions, and the Genocide Convention. The thrust of the argument was that non-state actors could violate the law of nations. Interestingly, the Second Circuit also cites Blackstone on piracy and invokes the concept of *hostis humani generis*, which, as we shall see later, plays a critical part in the evolution of the modern law of nations. The court reached the application of certain war crimes to Karadžić by holding Common Article 3 applicable to him and his band of followers. The circle was closed by holding Karadžić liable as well for private acts of torture provided they were committed in the furtherance of the other crimes, notably genocide. There were also allegations the defendant did act under colour of law of his would-be state Srpska. But for further litigation, the important side of the holding is the unequivocal commitment to the responsibility of individuals for the gravest possible crimes against international law.

7. TORTS AS DOMINATION

In the final analysis, the important point about *Filartiga* and *Karadžić* is that they bring to bear a clear paradigm of tort law, namely the defendant dominates a passive victim and acts aggressively against him or her. That is, even if there is no specific tort called torture, the account that we have offered of torture provides a general model for understanding tort liability. There are no torts based on the modern offences—genocide, war crimes, and crimes against humanity. Yet they all stand for the same paradigm of liability. They are to be contrasted with the other influential models of tort liability, which I have explicated earlier as the paradigms of efficiency and of reciprocity.[26] These other two models compete for influence in a wide range of tort cases that lie in negligence and strict liability. The model of efficiency requires a balancing of competing economic interests and a judgement of social welfare in order to impose liability. The paradigm of reciprocity focuses on the relationship of the parties and stresses the injustice of one side imposing a non-reciprocal burden on the other. In many cases of non-reciprocal risk-taking, the plaintiff and the defendant are engaged in a common transaction, but one which goes awry because one side suddenly increases the risk. This is the case with negligent drivers and negligent sportsmen.

Intentional torts can sometimes be analysed as cases of non-reciprocal risk-taking, primarily because intention in tort law is interpreted very broadly to include knowledge of substantial risk of harm.[27] But in the case of torture, the intentional infliction of pain or humiliation is hardly a matter of risk-taking. It is purposeful action, a one-sided transaction, a case of total domination.

Of course, the advocates of efficiency have their voice, even in the cases of torture and the general claim of necessity in the Rome Statute Article 31(1)(d). They claim that torture for a good cause is justified on the ground that the benefits outweigh the costs. Anytime someone suggests that a ticking bomb or other circumstances of necessity might have some bearing on the boundaries of torture, they are indirectly appealing to the paradigm of efficiency. This, as we have noted, was a view dominant for long periods of history. The movement today is towards absolutist thinking. This is true not only in torture, but in terrorism and in other war offences against the Rome Statute, such as the intentional killing of civilians, genocide, rape, persecution, and an as yet undetermined and under-analysed range of war crimes, such as declaring that no quarter will be given or depriving a defendant of a fair and regular trial.

We have good reason to take torture as the proper model for our thinking about liability under the ATCA for human rights abuses. *Filartiga* begins the modern process of development. Torture captures

---

[26] George P Fletcher, 'Fairness and Utility in Tort Theory' (1972) 85 *Harvard Law Review* 537.

[27] See, eg, *Garratt v Dailey*, 46 Wash 2d 197, 279 P2d 1091 (1955) (defendant, a young boy, pulled a chair out from the spot where the victim was about to sit down; held liable for intentional battery).

the tort paradigm of domination. The line of development is confirmed by *Karadžić*. Yet there is also room for doubts. First, we might wonder whether the absolutist thinking that governs our analysis of torture should prevail everywhere in the field. The Rome Statute provides a defence of necessity under Article 31(1)(d) but there seems to be no discussion of all of the crimes to which this defence might apply. It presumably does not apply to the grave breaches or to the offences in Common Article 3—ranging from killing civilians to depriving a defendant of a fair and regular trial. But no one knows for sure. The field awaits proper theoretical refinement. On this point, in particular—determining when the principle of balancing evils should apply and when it should not—there is much work to be done.

An additional problem is becoming clearer about the core cases of torture. I fault no one for not knowing whether water-boarding for short periods of time constitutes torture. We lack the most fundamental tools for assaying this problem. The language of the CAT is hopelessly misdirected. It would be good if we could follow the lead of Justice Barak in the Israeli torture case of 1999 and turn the question around. The issue should not be, 'what is torture?', but, rather, 'what are the permissible limits of interrogation?'. After all, there is no reason to think that the police or the military have the authority to do everything they want to do to detainees provided it does not fall within the taboo of 'torture'. The preliminary question is the authority of the police to impose any restrictive measure at all on a detainee. Interrogation is a justified police practice. But each instrument of interrogation must be justified by the extent that it contributes effectively to a sound interrogation, and no more force than is necessary for interrogation should be used. Earlier I conceded that in international law the focus should not be on administrative law but on the evil of the end result, which would imply that Barak's approach should not apply in ATCA cases. We should rather add a question mark to this proposition and await further analysis.

Should the burden for classifying a technique like water-boarding be on the person who seeks to condemn the action as torture or on the advocate who thinks that water-boarding can contribute effectively, without excessive cost, to the process of gathering information? It may be that criteria of efficiency slip back in by way of the back door of defining the core cases of permissible interrogation.

But even if we could follow Justice Barak's approach in the international legal analysis of torture, we have noted that the modes of analysis in international law are not the same as in domestic law. We cannot analyse the authority of the military as directly and easily as we can approach the authority of the police or the domestic intelligence services. The authority of the military is limited by the law of war, which is by derivation part of international law.[28] The law of war remains disturbingly independent of the domestic systems of executive authorisation.

In retrospect we can appreciate the boldness of Francis Lieber's taking on the problem of torture under the general heading of the limits on military necessity. He argued for the prohibition of torture 'to extort confessions'. But he had yet to comprehend the absolutist thinking that has come to the fore in the last few decades. It is not only perfidy and poison that are absolutely prohibited in the law of war and in international law generally. We have yet to think beyond torture to assess whether other offences—ranging from intentionally killing civilians to depriving defendants of a fair and regular trial—should be treated as absolutes offences, not subject to justification by claims of necessity. Torture should be our paradigm but we are in desperate need of a deeper theory.

---

[28] See the analysis of whether the crime of conspiracy constitutes part of the law of war in *Hamdan v Rumsfeld*, 126 SCt 2749 (2006).

6

The Jurisprudence of Sosa

The prolonged fight between Dr Alvarez Marchain and the US Drug Enforcement Agency (DEA) personnel has had an impact on the law of the ATCA as profound—at the risk of some overstatement—as the Civil War on the Constitution of the United States. Henceforth our thinking will be divided in pre-*Sosa* and post-*Sosa* phases of ATCA law. ATCA precedents that came before the second *Sosa* decision in 2004 constitute history. Even the language has changed. Most courts and scholars post-*Sosa* now refer to the ATCA as the Alien Tort Statute because that was the language used in the Supreme Court's opinion. For the sake of consistency, however, I have stayed with the term ATCA.

Most pre-*Sosa opinions* will survive only if appropriately cited and interpreted in the *Sosa* opinion. Everything that has happened since represents efforts to make sense of the mysterious language and reasoning used by the Supreme Court to save the ATCA within bounds it thought reasonable for future litigation about correcting human rights abuses.

But, as wars and political revolutions sometimes have effects other than those intended, whereas *Sosa* had the intention of curtailing the doctrinal foundations of the ATCA, in fact there has been more creative activity in expanding the applicable range of the ATCA in the last few years than in the decades from *Filartiga* to *Sosa*. The challenge of this chapter is to understand the *Sosa* saga in the courts and how the decision in 2004 could appear to be a severe cutback and yet covertly encourage expansion of liability under the ATCA.

1. THE ABDUCTION, AND LOSING IN THE SUPREME COURT

The clandestine activities of the DEA in Mexico and other Latin American countries can be expected to be the source of both good law and bad law.[1] In the particular story of Humberto Alvarez-Machain, the stage was set by a series of lawless moves by the DEA and their Mexican collaborators. The Mexicans had allegedly held a DEA agent captive in a house in Guadalajara where they tortured him and eventually killed him. Alvarez, as a physician, was allegedly present to supervise the torture and provide assistance where necessary. Allegedly, the DEA tried to negotiate the extradition of Alvarez with Mexican officials but they were unsuccessful. Eventually, on 2 April 1990, a group of Mexicans hired by the DEA kidnapped Alvarez from his office in Guadalajara, held him in custody in a motel overnight and then flew him to El Paso, where the Americans arrested him and took him to California to stand trial for complicity in the torture and death that had occurred earlier in Guadalajara.

Alvarez proved a tenacious adversary. He first tried to get the federal indictment dismissed on the ground that the abduction was an 'outrageous' violation of international law and. under the US–Mexican extradition treaty, the United States should be penalised for having taken forcible measures outside the framework of the treaty. In light of the common law principle that the presence of the body in court is sufficient to ground jurisdiction, regardless of how the body was obtained,[2] the claim of 'outrageous' abduction had little traction as a ground for dismissal. The majority conceded that Mexico might have a complaint against the United States for the violation of its territorial integrity but this possible violation of customary international law did not translate into a defence against prosecution. The government relied, successfully, on the familiar argument that treaties create rights for states but not individuals.

The government subsequently indicted Alvarez before a jury in Los Angeles. He was acquitted and then sought greater vindication by bringing an ATCA action against the government as well as the various individuals—among them *Sosa*—who had participated in

---

[1] In a case arising out of the same murder of a DEA agent in Guadalajara, the Supreme Court held that the Fourth Amendment to the Constitution did not cover 'unreasonable' searches and seizure occurring in Mexico: *United States v Verdugo-Urquidez*, 494 US 259, 108 L Ed 2d 222, 110 S Ct 1056 (1990). This case proved to be a problem to those asserting the application of the US Constitution abroad, in particular, in cases of detention in Guantanamo Bay. See *Boumediene v. Bush*, 127 S Ct 1478 (2007).

[2] *United States v Noriega*, 683 F Supp 1373 (1988).

his kidnapping. Again, he won in the district court on a summary judgment, and the Ninth Circuit confirmed.

The comprehensively researched and brilliantly reasoned opinion of the Supreme Court established the starting point for discussions on the ATCA for decades to come. The only problem with the decision is that the result is at odds with the rhetoric of the opinion. The justices were unanimous that Alvarez-Machain must lose his personal claim for a tort in violation of the law of nations. The exact reason that his kidnapping and involuntary cross-border transport did not express a norm of the law of nations remains to be considered. For the most part, however, the justices were unanimous that the ATCA has always been and shall remain a permanent figure in the US system for correcting the evils of human rights abuses.

One rarely encounters a decision of the Supreme Court in which the rhetoric points so affirmatively in one direction and the actual decision seems to represent the sacrifice of a single litigant so that many in the future will succeed. I will concentrate in these comments on the affirmative aspects of the opinion, and in conclusion offer some thoughts on how Alvarez's loss could be justified according to the theoretical structure developed in the early chapters of this book.

2. WINNING IN THE SUPREME COURT

For a controversial issue that had not been litigated in the Supreme Court for over two centuries, the Sosa case gained a surprising degree of consensus. All but two justices agreed on the preliminary issue of the Foreign Sovereign Immunity Act, namely that torts occurring abroad were barred under the Act unless the so-called 'headquarters doctrine' applied. All agreed on the interpretation of the ATCA as a jurisdictional claim grounded in the common law understanding of international law at the time the First Judiciary Act was enacted. The only difference between the six justices in the majority with Justice Souter and the three dissenters joining Justice Scalia is a jurisprudential dispute that was not really a proper matter for the court to ponder. My thesis is that when the misconceptions of language are stripped away, the unanimous consensus holds in favour of the ATCA establishing jurisdiction in the federal courts and permitting recovery under evolving norms of international law. There are some limitations that need to be imposed on this generalisation, but that are to be found, as I will show, in the theory of liability for torts.

The eternal puzzle for the courts in interpreting the ATCA is whether the statute is purely jurisdiction or whether it also creates a new cause of action. Just about everybody has agreed that the statute is jurisdictional, which leaves the puzzle as to what the applicable law should be. *Filartiga* solved that problem by invoking the evolving international law of torture for jurisdiction but then deferring to the district court to make a choice of law even without knowing whether torture was per se recognised as a crime or tort under the law of Paraguay. The approach of the Supreme Court in *Sosa* differs. The justices start on the assumption that the ATCA is jurisdictional, but not merely jurisdictional. It must also have reference to some body of substantive law. They were adamant that Congress had not created 'a jurisdictional convenience to be placed on the shelf for use by a future Congress or state legislature that might, some day, authorize the creation of causes of action'.[3] The court accepted the idea that the jurisdictional provision was enacted under the ambient international law of the time. And then relying primarily on Blackstone's *Commentaries*, published 20 years before the Judiciary Act, the court engages in a very sophisticated analysis of what that ambient law was.

We should note in passing that the court passes over a critical issue that concerned Judge Kaufman in *Filartiga*. If there is no diversity jurisdiction in a suit between two aliens, how does one justify the original 1789 version of the ATCA? *Filartiga* answered this question by positing that all claims under the ATCA arise under the laws of the United States. For reasons that we explore later, the Supreme Court today is chary of this argument. It is not willing to accept the simple syllogism that we set out. The idea that evolving international law is part of federal law is now subject to controversy.

What the court did accept is that the norms of recovery for ATCA claims should be found in the 'ambient' law of the time, in particular, as expounded by Blackstone. The argument that the

[3] *Sosa* at 719.

court should rely on Blackstone for an interpretation of the law of nations applicable in 1789 had its origins in Judge Bork's concurring opinion (not signed by any other judges) in the *Tel-Oren* case, denying ATCA liability for a PLO terrorist attack against Israeli civilians.[4] He insisted that the ATCA be interpreted against Blackstone's exposition of the law of nations, but he did not use the phrase 'ambient law'. Where that phrase comes from remains a bit of a mystery.

In order to explicate Blackstone's view of international law, the court first recognised the conventional Westphalian principle that international law creates rights and duties among states. The subject of the legal duty is the state as an organic whole, but primarily the executive and legislative branches. The judiciary is considered of lesser importance. Second, the court acknowledged that a whole dimension of international law attaches to individuals. They are initially defined as 'situated outside domestic boundaries' and 'carrying an international savor'.[5] However vague this may be, the reference is rescued by one indisputable example—the law merchant. The law merchant is interpreted broadly to include not only commercial transactions but also the law pertaining to shipwrecks and the 'status of coast fishing vessels in wartime'. The customary law on seizing vessels was familiar to the Supreme Court in light of its critical precedent, *The Paquete Habana*, which held that customary international law applied in the federal courts.[6]

But then the court went on to recognise a second division of international law as applied to individuals. This form of international law had a peculiarly common law bent. The court claimed that it exists because Blackstone defined three common law criminal law offences based on individual assaults with international overtones. The three offences are 'violation of safe conducts, infringement of the rights of ambassadors, and piracy'. They are listed on the well-worn page 68 of Volume IV of Blackstone's *Commentaries*. We should elaborate each of these.

---

[4] *Tel-Oren v Libyan Arab Republic et al*, 726 F2d 774, DC Circuit (1984) at 798.

[5] *Sosa* at 715.

[6] *The Paquete Habana*, 175 US 677 (1900). In this case the court found that the customary 'law of nations' declared coastal fishing vessels exempt from capture as a prize of war.

A safe conduct is a sovereign's guarantee to a merchant or emissary that he can pass over the territory and cross the frontier without interference. The principle of guaranteeing safe conduct has deep roots in English law. It is mentioned in the Magna Carta, as Blackstone reminds us.[7] A very famous case decided in 1473 in the Star Chamber—one of the most important in the history of larceny—testifies to the power of safe conducts as a trump on innovative decisions in the criminal law. Called *The Carrier's case*,[8] it was a dispute between a foreign merchant who had received a safe conduct from the King and the Sheriff of London. The merchant hired a carrier to transport some bundles of dyer's weed to Southampton. Along the way, the carrier broke into the bales and stole the contents. When he was arrested, the dyer's weed came into the hands of the Sheriff, who claimed that the bundles were to be treated as equivalent to feloniously taken goods or waif and therefore forfeit to the King. If there was a felony in the taking, the Sheriff should have won. Here are the legal moves back and forth between the foreign merchant and the Sheriff:

Merchant: no felony because the carrier had possession, and theft requires taking from the possession of another.
Sheriff: This is true but the carrier only had possession of the external wrappings, not of the contents, therefore felony.

The case is remembered on the basis of the Sheriff's argument. The case established the doctrine of 'breaking bulk', which was accepted as basic doctrine by the subsequent writers of criminal law.[9] In fact, however, the merchant won because he could assert his 'safe conduct' which the Star Chamber took to trump the general law of waif or abandoned goods. Fitzjames Stephen criticised the outcome as a concession to the royal interest in protecting foreign merchants.[10] He was absolutely right.

The second example in the Blackstone trilogy is 'infringement of the rights of ambassadors'. There is no reference to 'safe

---

[7] William Blackstone, *Commentaries on the Law of England*, Vol IV (Oxford, Clarendon Press, 1765) [*Commentaries*] at 68.

[8] YB Pasch 13 Edw IV, f 9, pl 5 (1473), 64 Seldon Soc 30 (1945).

[9] For a detailed analysis, see *Rethinking* at 66–70.

[10] 3 Fitzjames Stephen, *History of the Criminal Law of England* (London, Macmillan & Co, 1883) at 139.

conduct' in the Constitution but there is ample concern for rights of ambassadors. 'All cases affecting Ambassadors, other public Ministers and Consuls' are within the original jurisdiction of the Supreme Court. This was the critical clause that led to the court's accepting judicial review in *Marbury v Madison*.[11] Marbury tried to bring a writ of mandamus in the Supreme Court against Madison in his role as Secretary of State under President Jefferson. The Judiciary Act of 1789—the same statute that created the ATCA—permitted him to do this. Interpreting the clause permitting original jurisdiction in the Supreme Court 'in all Cases affecting Ambassadors, other public Ministers and Consuls',[12] the court ruled that Congress had exceeded its jurisdiction. It had always seemed to me plausible to read the reference to 'other public Ministers' to include high officials like the Secretary of State. But Marbury's complaint was a purely domestic matter (Madison refused to deliver the papers necessary for Marbury's judicial appointment, made under the previous administration). In light of Blackstone's emphasis on the international aspect of protecting the rights of ambassadors, the court was probably right to read the Constitutional reference to 'public Ministers' as those who were like ambassadors—for purposes of peaceable international affairs.[13]

Piracy too is mentioned in the Constitution. One of the specific powers granted to Congress is to define and punish Piracies and Felonies committed on the High Seas'.[14] There is no similar power with regard to defining safe conduct and offences against ambassadors. The reason is that piracies carry with them the customary baggage of peripheral offences, including trading with pirates, the master's absconding with the ship, and conspiracy to commit piracy.[15] The offence had so many branches and sub-branches that therefore congressional definition was required to know which acts would be punishable and which not. The violations of safe conducts

---

[11] 1 Cranch (5 US) 137 (1803).

[12] US Const Art III § 2, cl 2.

[13] Cf US Const Art II, § 3 (presidential duty to receive ambassadors and other public ministers). This clause carries overtones of an obligation towards other states, not towards domestic officers.

[14] US Const Art. I, § 8, cl 10.

[15] These are discussed in *Commentaries*, Vol IV at 71.

and torts against ambassadors were relatively well defined in the common law.

The important thing to note about the Blackstonian trilogy is that this is a distinctively English collection of common law criminal cases. In the case of the law merchant, we could expect other countries to replicate the English body of law governing international transactions. In the case of the trilogy, we have no proof that the US offences are anything more than an American projection of what international law should be like. We can surmise that other countries have crimes with contours similar to these three offences, but there is no reason to think that *The Carrier's case* would have come out the same way in another country and the contours of piracy probably differ from place to place as well. In any event, at the time the ATCA was enacted these offences could be said to be part of the common law with an international bent. In addition, these offences imposed individual responsibility on defendants. In that respect the criminal offences were like tort law and could be treated, with a little charity, as Blackstone's vision of the wrongful actions that would be recoverable in tort as violations of the law of nations.

The truth is that Blackstone had a very primitive conception of tort law. He devoted one of his four volumes to criminal law, but there is hardly a mention of tort law in the volume on private wrongs.[16] The reason was that the law of torts had still not transcended the debates about the particular writs. In 1773, Blackstone, as a judge on the Court of King's Bench, wrote a brilliant opinion on the difference between trespass and trespass on the case.[17] (The case is discussed in chapter one as 'the original ticking bomb case'.)[18] This is much better reasoned and more sophisticated than anything he writes about torts as such in Volume III of the *Commentaries*.

The difference between Judge Kaufman in *Filartiga* in 1980 and the nine justices of the Supreme Court in *Sosa* in 2004 is the way

---

[16] G Edward White does a heroic job trying to reconstruct a law of torts in Blackstone but the picture he presents is far more coherent than the text is itself: see G Edward White, *The Monsanto Lecture: A Customary International Law of Torts*, 41 *Val UL Rev* 755 (2006).

[17] *Scott v Shepherd*, 2 *Blackstone's Reports* 892, 96 Eng Rep 525 (1773) (minority opinion).

[18] See text above at ch 1 at pp 30–36.

in which their process of interpretation privileges the historical situation at the time of the ATCA's enactment. For Kaufman 'the law of nations' has an evolving set of references, as does any other branch of law. The meaning stays the same but the concept has differing contents at different moments of time. The nature of international law—in the traditional model, as a set of rights and duties binding on states—remains the same even though in 1950 official torture is not a violation of international law and in 1980 it is.

The emphasis on 'the ambient law' of the time expresses the new historicism that has overcome the increasingly conservative Supreme Court. No one ever thought that the due process or equal protection clauses should be interpreted against the ambient law of the time. No paragraph of the Constitution freezes in force the common law of 1789. If it did that, we could never conceive of the Constitution as a reformist document. Preserving history remains in constant tension with reform for the sake of sound principles of due process.

A good example of principle triumphing over history is *Bloom v Illinois*,[19] which tested the common law that a person accused of contempt of court could be convicted on the spot, without a jury trial. Bloom won his claim that for a serious contempt implying punishment of more than six months in jail, he had a right to a jury trial. Due process would mean nothing unless it stood for principles that went beyond the received practices of the time. The same is true about the law of nations.

It is true, however, that the Constitution is sometimes interpreted against the ingrained practices of the time. Even in *Bloom*, the court accepted the principle of a summary trial without a jury for crimes carrying minor penalties of less than six months in jail. There is no good reason but history for recognising this exception to the right to a jury trial. As in all fields, the claims of principle are constantly in tension with the claims of history.

In the last several decades, however, conservative forces have mounted an aggressive campaign in favour of a historicist and textualist view of the Constitution. The Constitution should be interpreted as it was written. The judges should eschew principle

[19]   391 US 194 (1968).

for the sake of the original will of the framers.[20] Judge Bork and Justice Scalia have been among the movement's champions.

The historicist school has led to a very peculiar mode of constitutional and statutory interpretation. The peculiarity is reflected in the idea of 'ambient law'. Let us assume that the intention of the framers and of the legislature is relevant to interpretation, perhaps even decisive as to the proper interpretation of a text. The question is whether the 'intention' of 1789 refers to a purpose to enact particular language as it was understood at the time (a defensible historical view) or whether this purpose includes within it the absorption of the surrounding legal practices of the time. For example, in 1868 the states ratified the Fourteenth Amendment, which forbids states from denying any person 'equal protection of the laws'. No one could quarrel with the propriety of the question, 'what did these words mean at the time?'. The more disturbing claim is that the language of the Fourteenth Amendment has built into it, as the ambient practices of the time, the practices that were then assumed to be compatible with the equal protection of the laws. In 1868 everyone assumed that schools in the North and the South would remain segregated. Integration of schools was not on their minds (indeed the ratifying states would have been shocked by the idea). We could say that officially endorsed segregation was part of the ambient law of the time and therefore incorporated by reference into the Fourteenth Amendment. But every lawyer trained in the United States would recognise this proposition as a betrayal of the constitutional mission. It would imply that *Brown v Board of Education*[21] was a misreading of 'the original understanding' of the principle of equal protection. Again the problem must be formulated as one of history versus principle. There are admittedly some aspects of the law of equal protection that are governed by history. Take, for example, the exemption of women from the military draft or the definition of rape as a crime of men against women. If these historical practices are still accepted, the strongest argument in their favour is simply tradition.

Now it would be possible for a legislator to prescribe that everything that is going on now should remain the law forever.

---

[20] See Bork's piece, 'Technological Innovation and Legal Tradition: Enduring Principles for Changing Times? The Challenges of Biology for Law, 4 *Texan Review of Law & Politics* 1 (1999).

[21] 347 US 483 (1954) (holding that segregated schools were inherently unequal).

This would be a peculiar form of legislation, and one that would ultimately be incoherent. How could one ever specify everything that is going on now? Still, the historicist argument remains that whatever is on the legislator's mind should serve as the guide to the purpose and the meaning of the statute enacted. Thus we find Justice Souter and the entire court subscribing to the following proposition:

> It was this narrow set of violations of the law of nations [that is, the Blackstonian trilogy], admitting of a judicial remedy and at the same time threatening serious consequences in international affairs, *that was probably on minds* of the men who drafted the ATS [the ATCA] with its reference to tort.[22] (emphasis added)

The court goes on to illustrate the 'ambient law' of the time with various cases that occurred during the revolutionary period. The history of these cases is well researched and convincing. There was an apparent need to provide a remedy to foreign plaintiffs in order to avoid international dissatisfaction with the infant Republic. Although the dangers of war might have been exaggerated, they did think of the ATCA as an instrument that would serve the peace.[23]

> The jurisdictional grant is best read as having been enacted on the understanding that the common law would provide a cause of action for the modest number of international law violations with a potential for personal liability at the time.[24]

The notion of the 'modest number' is the unwarranted leap. There is nothing in Blackstone or in the history of the time to support this conclusion. It would be like saying that the purpose of the Fourteenth Amendment was exclusively to eliminate racial discrimination against blacks (not against Chinese or Jews) because overcoming the slavery of Africans was on the minds of framers.[25]

The fallacy is to think that if X, Y, and Z are on your mind as a legislator, the statute you adopt must be limited to solving the problems of X, Y, and Z. Yet the addition of the words 'modest

---

[22] *Sosa* at 715.

[23] This argument has been in the air for the last 20 years. It provides a rationale for the International Criminal Court. The Rome Statute warns in its Preamble against the risks of not-punishing the crimes within its jurisdiction: 'Recognizing that such grave crimes threaten the peace, security and well-being of the world.'

[24] *Sosa* at 713.

[25] This proposition was, correctly, rejected in *Yick Wo v Tompkins*, 118 US 356 (1886), which held the equal protection clause applicable to discrimination against Chinese.

number' may have been the price of unanimity of the court. In the fourth part of the opinion, the historicists divided into two camps about how the ATCA should be interpreted today. Justice Souter wrote for the majority of the moderate five. Justice Scalia represented the let-it-be-as-it-was extremist wing. Making the jurisprudential positions of either side coherent is no easy task and in fact they both leaped from one philosophically dubious proposition to another. The differences between them go to the foundations of how we understand the way courts refine and develop the law.

3. DISCRETIONARY DEVELOPMENT OF THE ATCA

At the heart of Justice Souter's concern is how the court should engage in further development of the ATCA in a way compatible with the rule of law, the separation of powers, and the limited power of the judiciary. This debate about judicial law-making has been a preoccupation of US jurisprudence for the last 80 years. The argument fluctuates between views that are fictitious and those that are pure conjecture. The fictitious view is that judges are the 'mouthpiece of the law'. This is Montesquieu's famous phrase: *les bouches de la loi*. Judges do nothing but apply the enacted rules. The alternative view is that of course judges add something to the process of interpretation and application of the law but it is anyone's guess how much they do so. With all legal rules subject to speculation, there is no way to break down any particular decision between the input of the law and the input of the judge's personality. Actually, the critics of Montesquieu are right, but nobody knows how right they are (that is where the guessing comes in).

Philosophers may ponder these two alternatives but the truth is that the conundrum is not relevant to the work of judges. Their job is to apply the statutes, precedents, and commentary as well as they can. Outsiders can speculate about whether they are exercising discretion, and if so, how much. Reflecting about their own discretion is not the business of judges.

A generation ago there was a big debate among legal philosophers about whether judges use discretion in hard cases. The realists had said in the 1930s that judges exercise discretion all the time, by which all they meant was that judges bring some personal input to the process of decision. But we know of many rule-governed activities—all games of sport, for example—where the umpires apply the rules as fairly as they can. They do not choose the winner of the game.

Perhaps it was a mistake to use the word 'discretion'. The birthplace of the term is administrative law, which itself was taking shape at the time that the realists chose discretion as their primary concept.[26] Discretion (*pouvoir discretionaire* in French, *Ermessen* in German) in administrative law simply means that the judges enjoy a range of decisions without being subject to appeal. If they go to extremes, they are subject to reversal for 'abuse of discretion'. Their decisions, of course, are subject to criticism by their political superiors and by the public as a whole. They are supposed to pursue particular objectives—say, building roads and bridges in an attractive and safe manner. The broad scheme for their project is set by those higher up, but the contractors on the ground have to engage in fine-tuning. This is their range of discretion or choice.

When the realists adopted the term, all they meant was that the alternative—that judges are the mouthpieces of the law—was clearly wrong. They were right to reject the fiction that judges do nothing but apply the rules but they had no affirmative vision of how judges actually apply the law. HLA Hart entered the fray in 1961 and argued that the realists were wrong about the core cases of the law.[27] In the limited range where words had precise meanings, they had no discretion. In the penumbra of the law, yes, they did have discretion. According to this view, the law is something like baseball at its core but in the penumbra the rule is something like whoever runs the bases more elegantly gets extra points.

There are some situations in law that are based on precise rules like those in baseball. Take the rule against running red lights. There might be some disputes about whether the light was red or green when the driver crossed the intersection, but there there are

---

[26] Actually, one of the leaders in the field used the term 'discretion' as broadly as did the realists. See Kenneth Davis, Richard J Pierce, Barry R Pstrager, and Thomas Newman, *Administrative Law Treatise*, 10th edn (Aspen, CO, Aspen Publishers, 1993).

[27] HLA Hart, *The Concept of Law* (Oxford, Oxford University Press, 1961). See also Hart's 'Positivism and the Separation of Law and Morals' (1958) 71 *Harvard Law Review* 593.

also borderline cases in calling balls and strikes. It would not be quite right to say that police officers have the discretion to decide whether someone is liable or not. But they have the discretion to give tickets or not. Hart would have conceded all this, his point being simply that there are 'clear' cases of running red lights. Of course, the rules of the road differ in one important respect from baseball. The principle of necessity applies to justify running red lights in an emergency. There are no emergencies of this sort in the controlled and limited world of sports.

Ronald Dworkin launched his career by criticising Hart for conceding discretion in the penumbra of the rules.[28] By analysing the concept of discretion more deeply than any of his predecessors, he argued that judges never had discretion in the strong sense—namely where they are free to act as though they were legislators. Even if someone is running the red light in an emergency, there are firm criteria—principles, as Dworkin called them—for deciding whether the emergency is sufficient to warrant the danger to others. Because judges are obligated to apply these criteria, they have no discretion in the strong sense. They may have discretion in the weak and trivial sense that they must exercise judgement in applying the rule.

The key to Dworkin's move is a shift in the focus of discretion. For the realists as well as Hart, discretion is a spatial metaphor. It is broad or narrow—something like the width of a chute in which bulls must run. For Dworkin, it is matter of judicial obligation. If judges are required to take the measure of applicable principles, he claims, they have no discretion.[29]

The debate ended there. Dworkin convinced me but apparently not many others. He himself dropped the subject in his later work.[30] Lawyers continue to talk in the fashion of the realists. The received wisdom is that courts use discretion in interpreting the law. This pattern continues even though there is an obvious refutation of the claim that courts are like administrative agencies exercising discretion. The latter are subject to appeal only for 'abuse' of their discretion, that is, in extreme cases. Courts are subject to reversal

[28] Ronald Dworkin, *Taking Rights Seriously* (Cambridge, MA, Harvard University Press 1977).

[29] I have developed this point further in my article, 'Some Unwise Reflections About Discretion' (1984) 47 *Law and Contemporary Problems* 269.

[30] Dworkin, *Law's Empire*. (Cambridge, MA, Harvard University Press, 1986).

for every mistake in interpreting the law (provided that the mistake has a bearing on their decision).

Our problem is understanding what Justice Souter meant when he wrote in *Sosa*:

> [T]here are good reasons for a restrained conception of the *discretion* a federal court should exercise in considering a new cause of action of this kind.[31]

The use of the phrase 'new cause of action' may make the majority's comment seem like the recognition of judicial legislation. Perhaps Souter really meant that the court was doing something like engaging in legislation. He approaches the development of the ATCA with a sense of moral compromise—as though the court were transgressing the rule of law by recognising a claim for damages according to the statute. Thus he feels burdened with claims of modesty and the commitment to retain the same specificity and 'low profile' found in the Blackstonian trilogy.

The jurisprudence of the court's opinion goes from off-base to far off-base, illustrating the dangers of judges imitating their philosophical critics. The reason for restraint, Souter argues, is that our understanding of the common law has changed since the time of Blackstone. According to Holmes, the eighteenth-century writers thought of the common law as a 'a transcendental body of law outside of any particular State but obligatory within it unless and until changed by statute'. (This is not the self-understanding of Blackstone but rather Holmes' critique of Blackstone.)[32] Implicit in this view, Souter reasons, is the 'discovery' theory of the common law. Now we all concur that judges do not discover but make the law. This discretionary development of the ATCA must give due to regard to the function of judges as officials making the law.

The phrase 'judges make law' is a peculiarly American way of speaking. It turns on the ambiguity of the word 'law', a single word in English to refer both to the statutory law (*la loi*; *das Gesetz*) and to higher principles of law (*le droit*; *das Recht*). You cannot adequately translate the phrase 'judges make law' into a European

---

[31] *Sosa* at 725 (emphasis added).
[32] *Sosa* at 725 (citing Holmes' dissent in *Black and White Taxicab & Transfer Co v Brown and Yellow Taxicab & Transfer Co*, 276 US 518 at 533, 72 L Ed 681, 48 S Ct 404 (1928).

language. Of course, courts do not make statutes (law in the narrow sense). Nor do they make the principles that govern their actions (law in the higher sense). So it is safe to utter the untranslatable proposition that judges make law. The phrase has entrenched itself in our language as though it were an obvious empirical truth. In fact, it is but a play on the ambiguity of the word 'law'.

These expressions ('rule of law', 'discretion', 'making law') all belong to the same morass of bad jurisprudential estimates about how the law actually governs concrete cases. Justice Souter and the majority in *Sosa* were willing to tread on dangerous jurisprudential terrain. But their doing so has invited continuing confusion and outright hostility from some quarters on the bench—those who take the separation of powers seriously.

Uttering the word 'discretion' in the presence of Justice Scalia is like waving a red flag bidding him to charge. He had already gone on record in the *Chicago Law Review*[33] defending the rule of law as the application of rules as opposed to the free-ranging discretion of judges making law. This is not simply a theory of law for him but a democratic creed. The people define the law; the judges have no authority to usurp the people's domain by making decisions beyond the strict confines of the applicable rules. His language in his *Sosa* dissent is unusually suspicious of judges interpreting the law:

> "In holding open the possibility that judges may create rights where Congress has not authorized them to do so, the court countenances judicial occupation of a domain that belongs to the people's representatives.[34]

This remark brings a whole new dimension to the debate about judicial law-making. As the debate evolved from the realists to Hart to Dworkin, the theory of law could have applied either to democracies or dictatorships: it did not matter.[35] (And in those days, I believe, the debate was deliberately indifferent to the democratic nature of other governments, as is international law today.) Justice Souter seems to

---

[33] Antonin Scalia, 'The Rule of Law as the Law of Rules' (1989) 56 *University of Chicago Law Review* 1175.

[34] *Sosa* at 747 (Scalia dissenting).

[35] Hart made this clear in his debate with Lon Fuller in the 1950s. Nazi law—horribly bad law—was still law: HLA Hart, 'Positivism and the Separation of Law and Morals' (1958) 71 *Harvard Law Review* 593, and Fuller's response, Lon L Fuller, 'Positivism and Fidelity to Law—A Reply to Professor Hart'(1958) 71 *Harvard Law Review* 630.

be concerned about what the State Department might think about the court's awarding damages for human rights abuses and thus having a negative impact on our relations with other countries.[36] For Scalia the concern is just the opposite. The thought that customary practices abroad could defeat the preferences of the American people violates his conception of democratic self-rule. Thus he has rejected any critique of the death penalty based on what other countries do—notably the 'civilised' countries of Europe.[37]

The democratic theme derives from another critical aspect of Scalia's critique of the majority's opting for discretionary development of the ATCA. Discretionary development might be all right if the federal courts had the constitutional authority to do this. But, as he notes, neither the common law nor international law constitutes the supreme law under the Constitution.[38] Thus he question whether the federal courts have the authority to interpret the law of nations on the assumption that it has become part of the common law.

The critical precedent on the existence of the common law in federal courts is *Erie v Tompkins*, a 1938 decision that radically changed the rule of decision in diversity cases in the federal courts.[39] Until *Erie*, federal courts applied the common law as they understood it. This was the same common law that was elaborated by the great writers on the common law from Edward Coke to William Blackstone. The beauty of the common law is that every English-speaking country in the world adopted it. Of course, over time, differences of interpretation emerged. By 1938 there might have been one interpretation of contributory negligence in a state court and another in the federal court down the street. This was the problem that triggered the dispute in *Erie*. In diversity of citizenship cases, say for tort liability, the federal courts had no law to apply but the common law. But there was one exception stipulated by section 34 of the now much discussed 1789 Judiciary Act. The federal courts were required to decide according to the

---

[36] See the discussion of the South African litigation: *Sosa* at 733.

[37] *Roper v Simmons*, 543 US 551 (2004). Scalia did not specifically address the majority's repeated references to standards in Europe (also see *Thompson v Oklahoma*, 487 US 815 (1988)), instead focusing his arguments in both cases on the need for judicial restraint.

[38] US Const Art VI, cl 2 (Constitution, statutes, and treaties as the supreme law of the land).

[39] 304 US 64 (1938).

'laws' of the state in which they sat. The accepted view until 1938 was that the word 'laws' referred to the statutory laws of the states.[40] Where there was no statute and there were differing interpretations of the common law, the federal court was supposed to apply its understanding of the common law, as would any other common law court in cases not regulated by statute. The consequence was that the plaintiff could choose which interpretation of the common law was better for his case—that of the state court or that of the federal court in the same district.

The epithet 'forum-shopping' is often good enough to discredit a legal policy.[41] It was sufficient to cast doubt on the imagined possibility of plaintiffs' choosing between a state's common law and the common law of the federal court sitting in the same district. The jurisprudential attack on the traditional reading of section 34 of the Judiciary Act was Holmes' legal positivism. The new argument was that the word 'laws' in the Judiciary Act referred not only to the statutory law but also to the common law of the state. As the saying went, there was 'no federal common law'.[42] The very idea was sneered at—as equivalent to favouring 'a transcendental body of law'.[43] The implication under *Erie* was that the federal court had to apply the case law as well as the statutory law of the particular state in which it sat.

Of course, the law not only consists of cases and statutes but, as Dworkin reminded us in his critique of Hart,[44] it also contains general principles that guide the interpretation of statutes and cases. One of the problematic consequences of *Erie*—never discussed in the literature, so far as I know—would be that the federal court should also apply the principles recognised by the courts of the state in which it sits. So far as I know, no one ever successfully explained how the principles of law in California differ from those in Pennsylvania. Localising the common law to a particular sovereignty is not as simple as the positivists might think. Because prin-

---

[40] *Swift v Tyson*, 41 US 1 (1842).
[41] For another case in which it is invoked, see *Mapp v Ohio*, 367 US 643 (1961) (holding the exclusionary rule applicable in state courts under the due process clause, thus creating a uniform practice between federal and state courts).
[42] *Erie* at 78.
[43] *Ibid*.
[44] See *Taking Rights Seriously*, above n 28.

ciples appeal to us on grounds of their intrinsic merit, they are not so easily tied to the authoritative sources of particular states.

The reading of *Erie* had an enormous impact on the deliberations in *Sosa*. For Justice Souter and the majority, *Erie* represented the rejection of the discovery theory of the law. After *Erie* judges must be conscious of their role in 'making law'. Consciousness of this role should make them modest in fulfilling tasks such as the 'discretionary' development of the ATCA. In this position of the majority we find a curious mixture of Holmes' positivism and the free-for-all attitude of the realists who believed that judges always make law. It is worth noting that these two jurisprudential views are in fact incompatible. For the positivists, the rules and precedents dictate the outcome of future cases. For the realists, if anything dictates the outcome of litigation, it must be extra-legal factors, such as the 'felt necessities of the time'[45] or, the personal psychodynamics of the judge.[46]

Justice Scalia draws an entirely different inference from *Erie*—one that in my view has little support in Justice Brandeis' classic opinion in the case. Scalia thinks the question is one of constitutional authority. Whatever the general common law is or was—a transcendental body of law or judge-made law—the federal courts have no authority to apply it. Like the majority, Scalia assumes that now judges make law. They may not do this, however, if they must have no authority under the Constitution to do so. There are some specific areas, he admits, where the courts have created a body of precedent surrounding specific statutory schemes.[47] Scalia is willing to concede some kind of implied authority in these special cases but he is adamant that *Erie* represents 'the death of the old general common law'.[48] Again, '*Erie*'s fundamental holding [is] that a general common law *does not exist*' (emphasis in the original).[49] Admittedly, in this argument, the question of existence

---

[45] See Oliver W Holmes, Jr, *The Common Law*, ed Mark Dewolfe Howe (Cambridge, MA, Harvard University Press, 1963, originally published in 1881).

[46] Jerome Frank, *Law and the Modern Mind* (New York, Tudor, 1936).

[47] The classic example is the labour law typified by *Textile Workers v Lincoln Mills of Ala*, 353 US 448, 457 (1957).

[48] *Sosa* at 741.

[49] *Ibid* at 744.

gets a little confused with the question of authority. For example, it is possible that the common law still exists, even though the judges who apply it exceed their constitutional authority. Or they could have the authority in certain areas, but with no effect on the existence of a general or specific body of common law.

Scalia's reading of *Erie* in this way reminds me of the remark attributed to Thomas More in 'A Man for All Seasons'. When his prosecutors argued that he must be obedient to the King and sign the Act of Succession and pledge loyalty to the Church, he replied:

> Some men think the Earth is round, others think it flat; it is a matter capable of question. But if it is flat, will the King's command make it round? And if it is round, will the King's command flatten it? No, I will not sign.

The Supreme Court has a lot of power but it can no more rule that federal common law is dead than the King can declare the world flat. All the Supreme Court could do and all it did do in *Erie* was rule that the phrase 'laws of the several states' should refer to the common law as well as the statutory law of the state. Judicial decisions are matters of interpretation. Until 1938 one interpretation of the Judiciary Act prevailed. After 1938 another interpretation held sway. Judicial decisions are not about existence, any more than Parliament's decisions address scientific reality. Nothing prevents the Supreme Court from changing its mind once more and ruling that 'laws' in the Judiciary Act refers to statutory law, that *Swift v Tyson* was right after all.

The obvious counter-example to Scalia's jurisprudence is the practice of prospective overruling. The interpretation of the Constitution changes and sometimes the court holds that the ruling applies prospectively only,[50] but no one other than radical realists would say that the old Constitution is dead and a new one is born. The interpretation changes, and the interpretation may be made prospective only.

Scalia's view that the court can wave a piece of paper and declare the death of the common law leads him into an existential contradiction in interpreting the ATCA. He agrees with the majority opinion in the first three parts of Souter's opinion, which means that he accepts the theory that although the ATCA was jurisdictional it

---

[50] See *Linkletter v Walker* 381 US 618 (1965).

was not meant to be an empty shell. It incorporated the 'ambient law' of nations as understood by Blackstone. He subscribes to the basic Blackstonian trilogy: 'violation of safe conducts, infringement of the rights of ambassadors, and piracy'. Thus in his view the common law—incorporating international law—was alive and well in the early stages of the Republic. But then came the *Erie* decision, declaring the demise of the general common law. But the general common law was the seat of the international norms recognised in the Blackstonian trilogy. Thus Scalia is in the awkward position of believing that piracy was actionable under the ATCA before *Erie* but not afterwards. He tried to avoid this contradiction by arguing:

> Those accepted practices [referring to the customary international law reflected in the Blackstonian trilogy] have for the most part, if not in their entirety, been enacted into United States statutory law, so that insofar as they are concerned the demise of the general common law is inconsequential.[51]

Scalia's real target is the influence of international law on domestic law. He cannot abide the idea that the practices of other nations would influence the court in contested areas—the one always mentioned being the death penalty. He is at his best when he defends the autonomy of the US legal system on grounds of democratic self-rule. He is at his worst when he confuses national self-rule with the enforcement of private rights between parties both of whom are often not American.

4. RECONSTRUCTING THE *SOSA* OPINION

If we leave aside the superfluous jurisprudence reflections by both Justices Souter and Scalia, we can reconstruct a convincing opinion based on the premises shared by a unanimous court. We need only commit ourselves to the view that the ATCA was jurisdictional in nature but not meant to be an empty exercise of words. It incorporated the ambient law of nations as expressed in the three recognised cases—violation of safe conducts, offences against ambassadors, and piracy. We can assume that if any of the paradigmatic cases had been tried, the federal courts would have awarded

---

[51] *Sosa* at 749 (Scalia dissenting).

damages to a foreign alien. That law is binding on us today. We need not say anything about discretionary development of that original consensus. Nor do we need to pronounce on the meaning of *Erie* for a body of international law that was recognised as binding when the Judiciary Act was enacted. The job of the judges in assessing Alvarez's claim—as it is in any case of judicial reasoning—was to take the cases already decided and ponder whether they contain a principle that extends to a new situation. In the instant case, the problem was the unlawful abduction and kidnapping of Alvarez-Machain and taking him to the United States for trial. But the *Sosa* court was obviously concerned about the general principle of inferring applicable law from the principle underlying the Blackstonian trilogy.

The first thing to explore is whether a principle unites the original three 'precedents'—safe conduct, offences against ambassadors, and piracy, There must have been a reason that Blackstone chose these three cases as representative of the international law that had become part of the common law. They are not just three cases thrown together at random and appearing together on page 68 of Volume IV of Blackstone's *Commentaries*. One thing they have in common is that they all relate to effective diplomatic and commercial relationships among countries. Maintaining the basic grid of communication was essential for the flourishing of international trade and peaceful relations among countries. If something else proved to be a barrier to commerce, such as an illegal blockade, one would regard it, as well, as a violation of principle implicit in the trilogy.

These offences are not the most serious punished in the criminal law. They consist of assaults, thefts, and robberies. They are not in the same league, in domestic criminal law, as murder, rape, or treason—the crimes punished most heavily. Piracy, after all, is nothing but a form of robbery, in peacetime, on the high seas. And yet because it is dreaded by all sea-faring peoples, because it calls into question the possibility enforcing norms on trade routes, the pirate is considered *hostis humani generis*—the enemy of all humankind.[52] The same would not be said about the thief who broke open the bales and stole the dyer's weed thus violating the safe conduct granted to a foreign merchant.[53]

---

[52] The expression can be traced back to Sir Edward Coke (3 Inst 113).
[53] See above n 8.

The inclusion of piracy in the Blackstonian trilogy opens the way for an expansion of the principle towards other cases where the offender is considered *hostis humani generis*. This is the foundation of Judge Kaufman's thinking in *Filartiga*:

> Among the rights universally proclaimed by all nations, as we have noted, is the right to be free of physical torture ... [T]he torturer has become like the pirate and slave trader before him *hostis humani generis*, an enemy of all mankind.[54]

Piracy is the hinge case. From one point of view, it is simply the interference with commerce, no more serious than violating a safe conduct—if the court had allowed the merchant to recover his stolen dyer's weed. From the other point of view, piracy is the great evil that corresponds today to genocide and crimes against humanity. The critical move in the interpretation of piracy was the transition, as Kaufman suggests, from robbery on the high seas to the slave trade. This was a move made within the field of universal jurisdiction. Pirates could be prosecuted everywhere because no state could claim territorial or national jurisdiction. The leap to universal jurisdiction over the slave traders was of a different order. Although they functioned on the high seas, they were the nationals of a particular government and they violated the passive national interests of their victims. There was therefore a sensible basis for claiming jurisdiction on traditional grounds of a national connection. But the inclusion of slave traders in the category of those subject to universal jurisdiction signalled the moral shift. Originally, *hostis humani generis* might have had a purely procedural meaning—pirates were subject to universal jurisdiction because no single state could claim jurisdiction. As soon as slave traders were included under the label, the criterion became the moral nature of the offence. Thus it was but a short step in *Filartiga* from slave traders to torturers. The only problem is that the purpose of this development was not to interpret the Blackstonian trilogy but to create universal criminal jurisdiction to ensure that the worst criminals would not go unpunished.

None of these reflections is to be found in the *Sosa* opinions. Justice Souter adopts the above quote from *Filartiga* and thus accepts importation into the general law of nations of the criteria

---

[54] *Filartiga* at 890.

bearing on universal jurisdiction. This was perhaps inevitable because the court did not want to confront the question of principle underlying the Blackstonian trilogy. If they had done so, they have generated a totally different, and much more modest, theory. First of all, slave trading, which was permitted under the Constitution at least until 1808, could not have been seen as a violation of international law in 1789. And if the move is not made from piracy to slave trading, it is not entirely clearly how we support the moral transformation so clearly evident in *Filartiga*.

But this is all now history. *Filartiga* is indisputably good law—cited and quoted affirmatively four times by the Souter majority. If torture is a violation of the law of nations, then so too is genocide. And if genocide is violation, then so too are crimes against humanity and war crimes. All were sanctioned at Nuremberg and have now been written into the positive law—as spelled out in the Rome Statute. In effect, the court has been guided more by a paradigm of aggression, as initially expressed in the recognition of torture as the first modern offence compensable under the ATCA.

The implication is that international criminal law, as embodied in the Rome Statute, should be the guide for interpreting the Blackstonian trilogy in our time.[55] As Blackstone reasoned about the law of nations in the late eighteenth century, the third category of international law—the responsibility of individuals—should be based on internationally accepted principles of criminal law. The *Sosa* court endorsed Blackstone's analogy from criminal liability to tort liability. At the same time both the majority and the minority expressed a thinly veiled contempt for the way in which human rights lawyers have tried to read their expansive views into the law of nations under the ATCA.[56] The way human rights are stated in international conventions, a violation need not claim an actual

[55] The United States has not ratified the Rome Statute but its citizens are subject to liability for any crimes committed under the statute if the state on whose territory the crime is committed refers the case to the International Criminal Court: Rome Statute, Art 12(3).

[56] In the case of Justice Scalia the contempt is not so thinly veiled: 'The notion that a law of nations, redefined to mean the consensus of states on *any* subject, can be used by a private citizen to control a sovereign's treatment of *its own citizens* within *its own territory* is a 20th-century invention of internationalist law professors and human-rights advocates': *Sosa* at 750 (citing Bradley and Goldsmith, 'Critique of the Modern Position' (1997) 110 *Harvard Law Review* 815 at 831–7).

victim. The breach could be a prophylactic war crime such as declaring that no quarter be given.[57] In most cases, however, internationally criminal acts impose harm on large numbers of persons. Only those cases of actual personal harm, based on the paradigm of domination or aggression can generate tort liability.

The transformation of the ATCA from a tort primarily protecting international commerce to a tort embodying the general principles of compensation for suffering domination was outlined in chapter four. The nature of this transformation has not been properly understood. The courts and commentators were not aware of the principle protecting freedom of commerce expressed in the Blackstonian trilogy. Nor have they been aware of the way in which the law of universal jurisdiction, based on a moral theory of *hostis humani generis*, has gradually taken over the law of liability under the ATCA. The reason for this indifference to principle is that both the majority and the dissent in *Sosa* were bogged down in their false jurisprudential theories. They were too concerned about judicial discretion and whether judges make law to confront the actual principles at stake in the litigation.

In their mode of spatial discretionary thinking the *Sosa* majority was preoccupied by the danger of opening 'the door' too wide to the claims of human rights activists.[58] Thus the majority firmly express the concern that the only norms recognised under the ATCA be 'specific, universal, and obligatory'.[59] The channel is to be kept narrow and tight. We need to assess whether these spatial metaphors have practical relevance for future litigation.

5. DISCRETION AND SPECIFICITY

The requirements of universality and obligatoriness should be taken for granted.[60] No one would seriously assert a norm as part of the law of nations unless it is binding on everyone. That is all that is implied by the terms 'universal and obligatory'. The problem, therefore, is the concept of specificity.

---

[57] Rome Statute, Art 8(2)(b)(xxviii).

[58] The 'door' metaphor is used throughout *Sosa*, eg at 729 ('close the door', 'door is still ajar', 'vigilant doorkeeping').

[59] See below n 62.

[60] During the Cold War period there might have been a problem of communist and capitalist norms. Thus the Supreme Court would not rule that Cuba's expropriation

It is easier to cite examples of overly vague provisions than to define the concept of specificity. Good examples of elastic provisions are prohibiting 'unnecessary suffering'[61] or 'excessive harm'.[62] The *Sosa* court objected to treating the norms against false arrest and international kidnapping as sufficiently specific for liability. One wonders why. Perhaps the problem is that the time factor is elastic. Ten minutes of false detention would qualify as an international incident. The court was not about to place every police officer in danger of making a false stop that would qualify as a violation of the law of nations. The Restatement (Third) of Foreign Relations Law of the United States (1987), section 702, goes to the opposite extreme of requiring 'prolonged arbitrary detention' as a matter of state policy. The lack of specificity here is the accordion-like property of a 'prolonged' period of time.

There may be a broader point in the denial of Alvarez's claim that illustrates the way the paradigm of domination or aggression functions in tort law. As we should recall, the aggression is wrong because it falls on a purely passive victim, as in the cases of torture, genocide, and other basic human rights violations that cause harm. The victim of false arrest is not a passive victim. He or she interacts with the police in a way that results in an error by the detaining officer. The error consists, typically, in a mistaken assessment of probable cause to arrest, that is, in a mistaken assessment of the victim's conduct. The transaction is not one of domination, or at least not always. The arrestee often contributes to the transaction in a way that the victims of classic violations of international law do not. He or she may display more or less reason to justify a finding of probable cause. Admittedly, these factors do not speak to other disturbing features of the trial of Alvarez-Machain—for example his being abducted in violation of the extradition treaty with Mexico. Unfortunately, abduction of the suspect is one of the customary (though dubious) ways that common law courts acquire jurisdiction.[63] The abduction creates a claim between those nations

---

of the sugar crop was a violation of international law: *Banco Nacional de Cuba v Sabbatino*, 376 US 398 (1964).

[61] Rome Statute, Art 8(2)(b)(xx).

[62] *Ibid*, Art 8(2)(b)(iv).

[63] *Attorney General v Eichmann*, 36 *Israel Law Reports* 1 (1962); *United States v Noriega*, 683 F Supp 1373 (1988); *Ker v Illinois*, 119 US 436 (1986).

affected, in this case, Mexico and the United States, but not an individual claim of defence or for tort recovery. These factors together may account, in part, for the negative result of Alvarez's claim in the Supreme Court. The driving force may not be the language of 'specificity and universality' but rather the paradigm of tort liability that prevails in this field of law. We should at least keep our minds open to the possibility that the requirement of specificity is an illusion. I have more to say about this in the next chapter where I examine the actual law of piracy.

Understanding the use of these spatial metaphors of determinate and specific channels of the law requires that we understand the peculiar approach to discretion that the court has inherited from the realist tradition. If discretion is not regarded as room to manoeuvre but rather as a judicial obligation to weigh the relevant factors properly, the problem of specificity is much less troubling. In any event—apart from the result in Alvarez-Machain's own case, the jurisprudence of *Sosa* confirms that an enormous transformation has occurred in the foundations of the ATCA. It has moved from a modest body of law focusing on international commerce to a robust and multi-dimensional application of the moral criteria of universal jurisdiction in the name of protecting humanity against the worst wrongdoers.

But even the 2004 message of *Sosa* is about to change. The future of liability is not likely to be a surrogate for criminal trials, as it was in *Filartiga* and *Karadžić*. The future is likely to focus on tactical lawsuits directed against those who have funded the transgressions. In the future the emphasis of litigation will probably not be on establishing the liability of the principal wrongdoer but on collecting damages from those in a position to pay.

7

The Liability of Accessories

In the post-*Sosa* period litigators have discovered that the primary targets of litigation should be the suppliers and other facilitators of the human rights violations. Unlike the early days of *Filartiga*, *Tel-Oren*, *Karadžić*, and indeed *Sosa*—where the violators themselves were sued as defendants, the business of suing under the ATCA has become a search for defendants who can actually compensate victims. The purpose is not only to stigmatise the wrongdoers but also to collect handsome judgments from those who can afford them. This has directed attention to the corporate defendants who play an indirect role in most systematic human rights abuses. The resulting relationship is triangular—among P, D, and C. The plaintiff-victim P sues the corporate defendant C for having contributed to the defendant D's human rights violation. Thus P seeks to collect from C for facilitating the wrongs of D. Here are some recent examples from the case law.

1. Myanmar security services commit various alleged atrocities against local villagers while under the employ of Unocal oil company, which is building a pipeline in Myanmar.[1]
2. Alcoa and other chemical companies sell Agent Orange to the US army, which uses it in Vietnam to kill the vegetation providing the Viet Cong with camouflage. The toxic ingredients of Agent Orange also cause injuries to the civilian Vietnamese, who sue the chemical companies for compensation under the ATCA.[2]
3. Arab banks provide special accounts to subsidise the families of suicide bombers who attack and kill innocent civilians in Israel.

---

[1] *Doe v Unocal*, 395 F3d 932 (9th Cir, 2002), *vacated [by]* 395 F3d 978 (9th Cir, 14 February 2003).
[2] *Vietnam Association for Victims of Agent Orange v Dow Chemical Co*, 373 F Supp 2d 7 (2005).

The families of the victims sue the banks for compensation under the ATCA.[3]

4. Caterpillar, Inc sells bulldozers to the Israeli army, which uses them to demolish the houses of Palestinian families as a deterrence against members of the families acting as terrorists. Children killed by the bulldozers sue Caterpillar for compensation under the ATCA.[4]

5. C falsely swears out a warrant with the Zimbabwean police alleging the guilt of Cormick in illegal monetary transactions in Zimbabwe. The local police arrest and torture Cormick, who sues C under the ATCA for inducing the Zimbabwean police to use torture against him.[5]

The pattern in all of these cases is the same. A wrongdoer commits some more or less obvious violation of human rights (Myanmar security services, the US army, Arab banks, the Israeli Army, the Zimbabwean government). There might be a brief discussion about whether the violation is 'specific, universal, and obligatory'. Generally, that is not the problem in these cases. The US army uses poison against the Vietnamese.[6] The Arab suicide bombers kill innocent civilians. The Zimbabwean police engage in torture of their suspect. All of these are obvious violations of international law, but the legal action is directed elsewhere. Whether or not the wrongdoer enjoys legal immunity, the action is wrongful—a violation of the law of nations.[7]

The focus is on the corporate defendant or private individual who is involved in some way in the wrongdoing. The actual defendant might be the employer as in *Unocal* or the supplier of the materials used in the violation (the *Dow Chemical* or *Caterpillar* cases). The problem in all these cases is whether the relationship between the actual wrongdoing and the defendant is sufficiently close to justify liability.

[3] *Almog v Arab Bank*, 471 F Supp 2d 257 (EDNY, 2007).

[4] *Corrie v Caterpillar, Inc*, 403 F Supp 2d 1019 (2005).

[5] This case, *Christ v Cormick*, previously pending in the Federal District Court of Delaware, was a counterclaim by Cormick to Christ's claim for contractual breach. The plaintiff abandoned the claim for breach, which resulted in the dismissal of Cormick's ATCA claim.

[6] Hague Convention of 1907, Art 23(a).

[7] On the importance of the distinction between wrongdoing and culpability in criminal law, see *Rethinking* at 576–7.

In the past there might have a point in suing judgment-proof defendants in order to establish a moral point. In *Filartiga* and *Karadžić*, the point was made. Torture, genocide, and war crimes are violations of the law of nations. In the post-*Sosa* period, the focus has fallen on the corporate defendants who are in a position to pay damages for the enormous harm done. These are the cases where the action is today. The point of these suits should be as much to do well (by making money) as to do good (to make the right moral point). For the time being it does not matter who has won and who has lost in these particular cases. They all contain seeds for future victories in trial and appellate courts.

The problem in this area of the law is that although there are well-written briefs or opinions in all these cases, the entire field lacks a proper theoretical foundation. There is a very simple reason for this. We are discussing the field known in criminal law as complicity, or aiding and abetting. When can individuals who execute crimes become liable for employing, assisting, facilitating, advising, supplying materials or in other ways aiding and abetting the principal offender? This field has no clear history in international law and therefore some have expressed the opinion that the principle of aiding and abetting is not recognised in international law. One Supreme Court case actually holds that whether aiding and abetting is recognised as a mode of liability depends on legislation.[8]

'Aiding and abetting' is a term properly used in criminal law. This poses no particular problem for us, however, for the thesis of this book is that the ATCA must follow the contours both of tort law and of international criminal law in order to become the effective instrument for correcting human rights abuses it was meant to be.

Yet in the case law and literature there remains an extraordinary amount of confusion about two issues: first, whether corporate or other private defendants can be liable under the ATCA,[9] and second, whether liability for aiding and abetting exists under international law or, generally, under the ATCA. The first issue is settled at least with regard to private individuals. This is the point of the

---

[8] *Central Bank of Denver, NA v First Interstate Bank of Denver, NA*, 511 US 164 (1994) ('where Congress has not explicitly provided for aider and abettor liability in civil causes of action, it should not be inferred').

[9] *Nguyen Thang Loi v Dow Chemicals Co* 373 F Supp 2d 7 (2005).

Blackstonian trilogy, all of which hold private individuals liable under international law. Should there be anything special about corporate defendants? I could understand the problem if the analogy were drawn between corporations and state defendants[10] The issue here is not criminal, but tort liability, and for these purposes corporations are treated the same as private individuals in tort law all over the world.

Many countries still baulk at holding corporations liable for criminal offences; the reasons being that corporations do not act and cannot be guilty in the same way as natural persons. Only natural persons are liable under the Rome Statute.[11] The approach in Nuremberg was to pierce the corporate veil and hold the individual directors liable, say, for selling large quantities of Zyklon B to the administrators of death camps.[12] If aiding and abetting is a criminal law doctrine, and corporate liability makes greater sense in torts than in criminal law, then there might an argument against mixing apples and oranges. In order to understand the contours of the problem, we have to explore the contours of complicity both in criminal law and in tort law.

1. THE NATURE OF COMPLICITY

In the theory of criminal law the liability of the accessory (the aider and abettor) is a derivative of the principal's wrongdoing.[13] The principals actually execute the crime. The accessories play the lesser part of driving the car to the scene or providing the weapons, advice, counsel, encouragement, or back-up support. They are the supporting staff who make the crime possible. In German criminal theory, the accessory shares in the wrongdoing of the principal and yet both principal and accessory are judged and sentenced according to their individual culpability. Say, for example, the principal is excused by

---

[10] This seems to be the concern of some writers; eg Steven R Ratner, 'Corporations and Human Rights: A Theory of Legal Responsibility' (2001) 111 *Yale L aw Journal* 443.

[11] Rome Statute, Art 25(1).

[12] *United States v Krauch* (the *IG Farben* case) 8 *Trials of War Criminals* (1952, photo. reprint 1997) 1081 at 1152–3, relied upon in the Agent Orange case, above n 2.

[13] *Rethinking* at ch 8.

reason of insanity, duress, or personal necessity. The accessory can still be guilty on the basis of his own culpability. The common law generally shares these ideas but the principles are not made explicit.[14]

Another important difference between the two traditions is that German law punishes accessories at a reduced level, while the common law punishes all participants according to the same range of possible punishments. The degree of participation might, of course, influence the discretion of judges in sentencing decisions.

There are two difficult borderline questions. First, how do we distinguish principals from accessories in close cases. Suppose two people hold the victim while a third assaults him. Are the first principals or accessories? One solution is to call them co-perpetrators. Obviously this makes a tremendous difference in systems based on the German tradition, where the classification determines the level of punishment.

The other important legal issue is the lower threshold of complicity. A continuum of participation exists between those who are merely doing business and those who are doing business in way that significantly furthers a criminal enterprise. Selling Zyklon B as a delousing agent is an acceptable business; selling large quantities to concentration camps with knowledge of the implied purpose is not. This is the problem that haunts this field of law. And it does not matter whether we are attempting to define the lower threshold for the sake of imposing tort or for the sake of assessing the proper level of punishment.

The basic orientation of criminal law is that each offender should pay (be punished) according to his or her level of personal culpability. Tort law has a different focus. The primary question is not how much each defendant pays but ensuring that the plaintiff is fully compensated for his or her injuries. This correlates with other structural differences in tort law, such as the principle of joint and several liability, which renders each tortfeasor fully liable for the victim's damages.

Although tort law has institutions parallel to aiding and abetting and complicity, the language is different. The Restatement (Second) of Torts, section 876 recognises three ways that an 'accessory' can become liable in tort for the damages caused primarily by another.

---

[14] See *ibid* at 817–45.

One of these looks exactly like a standard of criminal facilitation: the 'accessory' is liable for the full amount of the damage if he or she 'knows that the other's conduct constitutes a breach of duty and gives substantial assistance or encouragement to the other so to conduct himself'. Although it makes sense to reduces the criminal penalty for accessories, tort law has traditionally been an all-or-nothing affair. If you are liable, you are liable for the full amount that you have caused.[15]

The threshold of complicity is a problem in every legal system. The accessory must have some impact on the execution,[16] and critically, the impact must stand out from the background conditions of normal social services. For example, a gas service attendant does not become liable for a crime just because he knows that a few bank robbers need to fill up in order to reach their destination. Hitler's secretaries who lived with him in the bunker and who typed all his letters and thus knew everything that was going on were not considered accessories in crimes against humanity.

A pair of US federal cases illustrate the distinction nicely. In the leading case in this field, *United States v Falcone*, the Second Circuit held that as a matter of law the supplier of sugar to a distiller was not guilty—despite his knowledge of the illegal purpose—of joining the illegal organisation of distillers. As Learned Hand formulated the guiding principle of American law:

> It is not enough that he [the seller] does not forego a normally lawful activity, of the fruits of which he knows that others will make an unlawful use; he must in some sense promote their venture himself, make it his own, have a stake in its outcome.[17] (emphasis added)

The critical term here is 'stake in the outcome'. The partner case to *Falcone* is *Direct Sales v United States*,[18] in which the Supreme Court unanimously affirmed the conviction of a seller of morphine

---

[15] For the new trend to apportion liability based on 'market share', 'lost chance', and other theories, see *Sindell v Abbot Laboratories*, 26 Cal 3d. 588, 163 Cal Rptr 132 (1980), *cert denied* 101 US SCt 286 (1980). These developments are compatible with full liability for the portion of the harm caused.

[16] The Model Penal Code (MPC) has attempted to define a crime of attempted complicity: MPC § 2.06(a)(ii) ('aids or agrees or attempts to aid such other person'). This proposal was apparently not accepted in Rome Statute, Art 25(3) on complicity.

[17] *United States v Falcone*, 109 F2d 579 (1940) at 581.

[18] 319 US 703 (1943).

to a ring of illegal users. There were two factors that distinguished the case from *Falcone*: (1) the seller 'stimulated' the sales to buyer and therefore had an economic 'stake in the venture', and (2) the item being sold was regulated and dangerous in itself. The court drew an analogy between the sale of morphine and the sale of machine guns. The latter point is highly relevant for ATCA litigation. When the supplier is not selling sugar but Zyklon B or Agent Orange, the threshold of liability should be easier to satisfy.

Those who fall below the threshold of liability can claim that they are engaged in the ordinary course of business. They are background actors—whatever their knowledge of the wrongdoer's purposes might be. The concept of a 'stake in the outcome' is a useful way of marking the boundary between ordinary business and criminal facilitation. When a supplier like IG Farben supplies sufficiently large quantities of Zyklon B to kill thousands of people, it obviously has an economic stake in the outcome. If as a result of a personal grudge, C falsely swears out a warrant against Cormick with the expectation that Cormick will be tortured, C has a personal stake in the outcome. In the Arab bank case, the providing of banking services to suicide bombers and their families was based on a stake informed by ideological hatred and loyalty to a terrorist movement. On the other hand, Caterpillar's sale of bulldozers to the Israeli army may not have reached the percentage of their total sales to imply that they had a stake in the use of these bulldozers to demolish Palestinian houses.

Where the corporate defendant has an economic or a personal, ideological stake in the venture, the objective threshold is fairly easily satisfied. Then there might be some dispute about the exact subjective requirement to satisfy the criteria of liability. Of course, the corporate supplier must know of the illegal purpose. This knowledge is readily inferred from the excessive quantities supplied. The problem is whether the corporate supplier must display a collective purpose to further the violation of human rights.

This is a contested area. If tort law were to follow criminal law strictly, it might adopt a test comparable to the Model Penal Code, which requires that an accomplice act 'with the purpose of promoting or facilitating the commission of the offense'.[19] In

---

[19] MPC § 2.06(3)(a).

this context it should make a difference whether we are discussing criminal or tort liability. The criminal standard is pitched to individuals for whom these fine gradations of knowing and intending make a difference. In the context of corporate tort liability the most we can hope for is common knowledge that corporate activity will have the effect of facilitation of the criminal activity. The Rome Statute focuses on individual criminal liability and therefore requires a 'purpose of facilitating the commission of the offense'.[20] In the case of complicity in tortious wrongdoing it should be sufficient that the corporate defendant actually contributes to the result with the knowledge that its actions are likely to have contributed to that end. This is the way the court in *Almog v Arab Bank* expressed the subjective requirement of the offence:

> The standards for aiding and abetting liability discussed above do not require that Arab Bank had the specific intent to cause the specific acts which injured plaintiffs; under ... the general standards of aiding and abetting liability it is sufficient that Arab Bank acted intentionally and with knowledge that its conduct would ... facilitate the underlying violations when it engaged in the acts alleged.[21]

This is the correct standard for testing the complicity of corporations in violating international legal normcs. The officials of the bank need not have the same criminal purposes as the principal wrongdoers but they must provide them with services knowing that this will facilitate the wrongdoing.

2. THE *KHULUMANI* CASE[22]

The last case in the series supporting corporate liability for complicity is perhaps the most dramatic and sophisticated in its legal argument. The case is the culmination of the long dispute about whether prudential, diplomatic considerations should preclude judicial adjudication of the claims of hundreds of victims of apartheid against 50 corporations that were allegedly complicit in the maintaining the regime. The Supreme Court in *Sosa* hinted that it disfavoured

---

[20] Rome Statute, Art 25(3)(c).

[21] *Almog v Arab Bank*, 471 F Supp 2d 257 at 291 (EDNY, 29 January 2007).

[22] *Khulumani v Barclay National Bank*, 504 F3d 254 (2d Cir, 12 October 2007).

the South African litigation as part of its analysis of the prudential considerations influencing the exercise of the court's discretion: A judicial proceeding in the United States could arguably interfere with the respected Truth and Reconciliation Commission in South Africa. This concern was expressed in footnote 21 of the *Sosa* opinion, which advises the lower courts to engage in 'case-specific deference to the political branches'. The political branches both in the United States and in South Africa wanted to keep the US courts out of the litigation. Judge Katzmann dismissed this effort to antici-pate and control future litigation with a crisp one-liner: 'We view summary dismissal at the behest of a footnote as premature.'[23]

The more dramatic feature of Judge Katzmann's concurring opinion for the Second Circuit is that he completely endorsed the theory of this chapter that the evolution of the ATCA has instinc-tively and properly followed the development of international criminal law. It begins with the Blackstonian trilogy and then builds on the moral opening provided by piracy and the concept of *hostis humani generis*. Piracy leads to torture, and eventually to all of the crimes of defined by the Rome Statute—genocide, war crimes, and crimes against humanity. The entire Rome Statute and even the case law of the ad hoc tribunals becomes part of the customary international law determining the norms sufficient for jurisdiction under the ATCA. It goes without saying that the provi-sion in the Rome Statute on complicity (Article 31) is also included in the evolved international law recognised under the ATCA. As a result there is no serious issue about whether private parties can be held to be accessories under the ATCA properly understood.

Actually there should never have been a serious issue about whether private parties could be liable for aiding and abetting violations of international law. The Blackstonian trilogy was held to be the highest authority on this issue. Judge Katzmann's extensive discussion of piracy includes abundant material on complicity. Blackstone lists about a dozen different ways of aiding and abetting piracy, including 'running away with any ship, boat, ordnance, ammunition, or goods; or yielding them up voluntarily to a pirate; or conspiring to do these acts'.[24] Anyone engaging in

---

[23] *Ibid* at 251.
[24] *Commentaries*, Vol IV at 72.

these acts shall 'be adjudged a pirate, felon, and robber, and shall suffer death, whether he be principal or accessory'.[25] In the face of piracy we are not entirely sure what it means for an offence to be 'specific' or 'well-defined'. In the one major prosecution for piracy in the nineteenth century, the court expatiates for pages about the twists and contours of the offence.[26] With a sufficient degree of commentary, every offence is well defined. Oddly, the *Sosa* court claims that this kind of detailed discussion reflects 'the specificity with which the law of nations defined piracy'.[27]

In any event, there are many ways to reach the conclusion that private parties are subject to liability under the ATCA for aiding and abetting a primary offence. Whether corporations can be liable depends only on how seriously we take the analogy from criminal law to tort liability. Criminal law can inform the analysis of the ATCA, as it has done in *Sosa* and in its aftermath. But it would be equally convincing to reason directly from principles of complicity in tort liability. In his concurring opinion in *Khulumani*, Judge Hall relies more heavily on section 876 of the Restatement (Second) of Torts. The provision recognises that one individual is liable for the harm caused by another if, among other things, he or she:

> knows that the other's conduct constitutes a breach of duty and gives substantial assistance or encouragement to the other so to conduct himself.

It is worth noting the difference between the ways criminal lawyers and tort lawyers think about complicity. For criminal lawyers, the accessory is 'legally accountable' for the conduct of another.[28] In tort cases, the accessory is liable not for the conduct but directly for the harm to the victim. The consequence is that if the accessory is merely negligent, he or she might be liable for actions triggered by his creating an unreasonable risk, for example, if a seller provides the buyer with a dangerous product. Complicity in criminal law requires an intention to facilitate the criminal plan. Under tort law,

[25] *Ibid.*
[26] That is, *United States v Smith*, 18 US 153, 5 Wheat 153, 163–80, 5 L Ed 57 (1820).
[27] *Sosa* at 732.
[28] See, eg MPC § 2.06(2).

one person can be liable for the harm caused by another simply by increasing the risk that the harm will occur. The latter is not really a form of complicity but rather a means of imposing direct liability for excessive (negligent) risk-taking.

The disadvantage of relying on tort law in this context is that wrongs in tort, typically, are local affairs; they do not violate the law of nations. The truth, however, is that criminal violations are also typically local matters. That is why, under the Sixth Amendment, they must be tried 'by an impartial jury of the State and district wherein the crime shall have been committed'. Blackstone happened to pick three examples of criminal violations that had an international reach. The new offences, included since *Filartiga*, are, of course, of international significance.

The *Khulumani* case turns out to be a magnificent laboratory for comparing the approaches of criminal law and tort liability to accessorial liability. The approach of criminal law, as endorsed by Judge Katzmann, is based on a more nuanced body of law. But the tort approach, advocated by Judge Hall, has the advantage of side-stepping possible qualms about holding corporations liable under principles of criminal law.

The important point for both approaches is that the immunity of the primary offender need not stand in the way of accessorial liability. This point is well established in the theory of criminal law because complicity is based on the wrongdoing of the offender. This point is less likely to be approached in thinking about tort liability for facilitation. Yet liability for harm done should not be affected by the immunity of a co-perpetrator. In addition, since the Blackstonian trilogy, *Filartiga* and *Sosa*, the focus of ATCA liability has been on criminal offences. We can expect that in the future, the criteria for secondary liability will—in line with the opinion of Judge Katzmann—also conform to the theory of criminal liability.

8

Concluding Theses

It is worth summarising here the well-defined claims that have emerged in the course of this study. Some of these claims were left implicit in the course of the analysis. Now we underscore their importance.

1. The concept of 'tort' as used in the ATCA is not limited to the historical significance of torts in the eighteenth century. No judge has attempted to apply the principle of historical and textual reading to limit the concept to what Blackstone may have intended by the term. Therefore the notion of torts, as used in the ATCA, is to be understood as the concept has evolved over time.

2. The concept of 'torts' in the common law is broader in the modern common law than in the civil law tradition, all of which have an analogous concept of extra-contractual liability. Tort law in the common law tradition includes product liability, medical and legal practice, and fault-based injuries that occur in the course of business relationships. Most of these are considered 'contract' in French and German law.

3. The law of torts, in general, is informed by three archetypes of liability—the paradigms of efficiency, reciprocity, and aggression. The former expresses the principle of cost–benefit analysis, both in the analysis of negligence and in taking the aim of the system as a whole to be the optimal management of accidents. The second accounts for the traditional principles of the law of torts found in all major legal systems. These include the principles of fault, contributory fault, strict liability, and proximate cause. The third is the appropriate model for analysis of ATCA liability. It represents that part of tort law, primarily intentional torts, that is most directly influenced by the criminal law. The basic model is one of domination or aggression by the offender over a passive victim.

4. The modern approach to the ATCA begins with *Filartiga*, which recognises state-sponsored torture as a violation of international law, even as applied to the state's own citizens. The remarkable feature of the case is that it imposed liability in the case of one alien suing another about an incident that occurred abroad. There was no tie to the United States except service of process on the defendant.

5. Torture perfectly captures the tort paradigm of domination or aggression. The victim is the passive object of the aggression. The only question about the recognition of torture as the first modern case under the ATCA is the problematic limitation of liability to state-sponsored torture. There is no obvious reason or principle for excluding torture by private parties.

6. *Karadžić* completed the transition to the modern jurisprudence of the ATCA by imposing individual liability for genocide, crimes against humanity, some war crimes, and torture so far as it contributed to one of these other offences. The additional list of offences—rapidly expanded from *Filartiga* to *Karadžić*—all conform to the paradigm of aggression. The victim is the passive object of domination, either by the state or a group of non-state aggressors.

7. *Sosa* shifted the focus of analysis from acts that were evil in themselves—for example, torture, genocide—to the Blackstonian trilogy of cases that impeded the flow of international commerce. The reasoning was that the ATCA was a jurisdictional provision that invoked the ambient international law of the time, so far as it was incorporated into the common law. The development of the ATCA was left either to the discretion of the court (per the majority) or frozen at its inception (per Scalia). Neither side paid much attention to arguments of principled development of the law based on the Blackstonian trilogy. At the same time *Sosa* enthusiastically endorsed both *Filartiga* and *Karadžić*. The only loser in the *Sosa* case was the plaintiff himself. And that is partially explained by the interaction between the arrestee victim and the arresting officers. This is not a simple case of domination. It does not conform to the paradigm influencing recovery in the standard line of cases from torture to genocide to terrorism and, finally, to apartheid.

8. *Sosa* stressed that the norms to be applied in the future would have to be specific and determinant—as well as universal and binding. These terms are not to be taken literally. They are a reflection of the jurisprudential style of the *Sosa* opinion, one which focuses on spatial metaphors rather than on the principles underlying the judicial development of the law. The discussion of piracy in Blackstone and the case law on piracy indicate that with sufficient qualification and explanation every norm in international law is sufficiently specific to warrant liability. The cases likely to be on the borderline of liability are those where the relevant norm contains an elastic time clause or those which are premised on an interaction between the victim and the offender.

9. The last two cases discussed—*Arab Bank* (terrorism) and *Khulumani* (apartheid)—arise in the context of cases imposing liability on the corporate facilitators of the human rights abuses. These cases represent the ATCA of the future. In the future there will be little point in duplicating the work of the ICC by suing the wrongdoers of mass atrocities. The challenge for lawyers will be to locate the corporate sponsors who fund these abuses, provide essential services, make a profit, and have a 'stake in their outcome'. The guiding principles will be international criminal law, with the single modification that liability will attach to corporate as well as individual accessories.

10. The major questions left open for the future are the possibility of justification under Article 31(1)(d) of the Rome Statute and the ever-present argument that the claims are not justiciable because they interfere in the domestic affairs of foreign governments. Judge Katzmann rejected these concerns in *Khulumani*, but the (partially) dissenting Judge Korman devoted his entire concurring opinion to this theme. History has shown constant division of the judges on the right approach to the ATCA. There will be always be dissenters, but the main lines of thought support the thrust of the *Almog* and *Khulumani* cases. The courts are ready, willing, and able to hold corporate accessories liable for the wrongdoing they promote in their pursuit of business. This will be the way we correct evil in the twenty-first century.

APPENDIX ONE

ATCA Cases Cited in the Preceding Text in the Order they were Cited

JOSE FRANCISCO SOSA, Petitioner v HUMBERTO ALVAREZ-MACHAIN *et al*; UNITED STATES, Petitioner v HUMBERTO ALVAREZ-MACHAIN *et al*, 542 US 692; 124 S Ct 2739; 159 L Ed 2d 718 (2004) (*Sosa v Alvarez-Machain*)

The Supreme Court ruled that the plaintiff, who had been seized by a Mexican national at the request of the DEA, could not bring an action under the ATCA because his alleged arbitrary arrest did not constitute a violation of the law of nations. In the plurality opinion, Justice Souter held that claims under the present-day law of nations must rely upon 'a norm of international character accepted by the civilized world and defined with a specificity comparable to' the eighteenth-century notion of piracy. To determine violations of the law of nations under the ATCA, one must look at the 'ambient law' of 1789. (See a more detailed discussion of this in chapters five and six.) Causes of action must allege a violation of a 'definable, universal, and obligatory [international] norm.' Courts should consider the implications of recognising any new cause of action, both on the courts as well as on foreign policy, and serve as 'vigilant doorkeepers' to ensure that only a narrow class of international norms be recognised under the ATCA. The Court was open to recognising claims against individuals for violations of the law of nations irrespective of any state involvement.

Justice Scalia, in a concurring opinion joined by Justices Rehnquist and Thomas, objected to any expansion of the ATCA beyond the originally identified causes of action of: violation of safe conduct, infringement of the rights of ambassadors, and piracy.

Justice Breyer, in a concurring opinion, stated that the courts should also consider the 'notions of comity' with foreign states when deciding on the recognition of a new cause of action under the ATCA.

DOLLY ME FILARTIGA and JOEL FILARTIGA, Plaintiffs–Appellants v AMERICO NORBERTO PENA-IRALA, Defendant–Appellee, 630 F2d 876 (1980) (*Filartiga v Pena-Irala*)

In this Second Circuit Court of Appeals case, the Court over-turned a district court dismissal for lack of jurisdiction under the ATCA. The plaintiffs, residents of Washington DC, were the father and sister of an alleged 17-year-old victim of torture and murder in Paraguay. There were no jurisdictional ties between the United States and the alleged offence except that service of process on the defendant occurred in the United States. The defendant argued that, since the plaintiff had a legally recognised cause of action in Paraguay for this conduct, it would be incorrect for the US courts to assert jurisdiction. The Court held that the ATCA, though not granting new rights to aliens, did serve to open the federal courts for adjudication of internationally recognised rights. Using United Nations declarations and scholarly opin-ions as evidence, the Court found torture to be a clearly defined violation of international law and thus an appropriate basis for cause of action under the ATCA. (The Court held that, when identifying violations against the law of nations, one must look to current international law *vice* the law of 1789, and that torture had become like piracy and slavery: crimes against mankind as a whole). However, the Court implied that Paraguayan law should be applied to the substance of the issue, which would appear to operate as an obstruction to proving liability. (See the beginning of chapter five for a detailed discussion of the opinion in this case.) Under local law, civil recovery would only be permitted fol-lowing a criminal conviction, which was doubtful, since another individual, in an allegedly staged proceeding, had confessed to the crime.

S KADIC *et al*, Plaintiffs–Appellants v RADOVAN
KARADŽIĆ, Defendant–Appellee; JANE DOE I and
JANE DOE II, Plaintiffs–Appellants v RADOVAN KARADŽIĆ,
Defendant–Appellee, 70 F 3d 232 (1995) (*Kadic v Karadžić*)

In this Second Circuit case, the Court reversed and remanded a
claim dismissed by the district court. The plaintiffs alleged that
the defendant, as the leader of militia forces in a region of Bosnia-
Herzegovina, had directed and exercised control over military
forces in a campaign of genocide, rape, forced prostitution and
impregnation, torture and other cruel inhuman acts against the
ethnic Bosnian and Croat population in the area. The lower court
had dismissed the case on the ground of lack of subject-matter
jurisdiction because the alleged acts were committed by non-state
actors. The Court held that the 'violation of the law of nations' element of an ATCA claim did not require state action for all alleged
offences. Specifically, it recognised that genocide, war crimes under
Common Article 3 of the Geneva Conventions, and acts of torture
that were included within the crimes of genocide and war crimes
constitute violations of the law of nations that do not require state
action to incur liability under the ATCA. On non-genocidal/war
crime torture, summary execution and the other offences alleged,
the Court held that the plaintiffs should have the opportunity to
prove that the region led by the defendant, Srpska, did merit state
status under the law of nations, or alternatively, that the defendant
was acting in concert with the state of Yugoslavia.

HANOCH TEL-OREN, IMRY TEL-OREN, *et al*,
Appellants v LIBYAN ARAB REPUBLIC *et al*, 726 F.2d 774
(1984) (*Tel-Oren v Libyan Arab Republic et al*)

This DC Circuit case affirmed the lower court dismissal in three
concurring opinions. The plaintiffs alleged that the defendants
were complicit in a series of attacks and torture committed by PLO
members against Israeli, American and Dutch civilians on a day
trip in 1978.

   In a concurring opinion, Judge Edwards (disagreeing with the
opinion of Judge Bork) held that the plaintiffs need not show that
international or treaty law must specifically identify a private right

of action in order for suits to be brought under the ATCA. The ATCA includes within it a right to sue. Using domestic law as a basis, Edwards held that alleging a common law tort that violates the law of nations avoids the issues of diversity or amount-based jurisdiction. The violations of the law of nations are not frozen from the time of enactment (limited to piracy, acts against the rights of ambassadors, and violations of safe conduct). Judge Edwards, defending and using the ATCA principles outlined in *Filartiga*, found that the law of nations holds non-state actors to a lesser standard than state actors, and thus held that the plaintiffs had not alleged a justiciable violation of the law of nations. Torture is only actionable if it is 'official torture', and the PLO is not a recognised state actor. Further, allegations of terrorism cannot be recognised as clear violations of the law of nations. In a second concurring opinion, Judge Bork argues that separation of powers mandates a reading of the ATCA that would require an international law grant of a right to sue; it is incorrect to hold that there is an implied right to sue within the ATCA. Further, causes of action under the ATCA are limited to the recognised offences at the time of enactment: piracy, acts against the rights of ambassadors, and violations of safe conduct. In his concurring opinion, Judge Robb reasons that the case must be dismissed because it is based on a non-justiciable political question touching 'on sensitive matters of diplomacy'.

SHAFIQ RASUL *et al*, Petitioners v GEORGE W BUSH, PRESIDENT OF THE UNITED STATES, *et al*, 542 US 466 (2004)

The ATCA was a side issue in this important case on the use of habeas corpus to test the legality of offshore military detention. The plaintiffs alleged that they were improperly detained in violation of the law of nations. They were captured by US military forces overseas and then moved to the military base at Guantanamo Bay, Cuba. The defendant argued that the World War II case law, primarily *Eisentrager*, had recognised an exception for prisoners in military custody overseas denying them access to the writ of habeas corpus. Supporting the opposite result, Justice Kennedy held that the practical sovereignty of the United States over the Guantanamo

Bay prison and the indefinite nature of the plaintiffs' detention, without any level of adjudication concerning status, distinguished the present situation from the facts of *Eisentrager*.

ABDUL-RAHMAN OMAR ADRA v VIRGIL A CLIFT and NESRINE CLIFT, 195 F Supp 857 (1961) (*Adra v Clift*)

The District of Maryland Court in this case dismissed a claim for custody of a minor child filed under the ATCA. The plaintiff alleged that the defendant illegally denied him physical custody of their minor daughter in violation of a Lebanese custody order. Further, he alleged that the defendant had illegally secured his daughter's entry into the United States through a fraudulent use of a passport. The court found jurisdiction over the claim, ruling that the fraudulent use of the Iraqi passport was a violation of the law of nations and that a suit for custody could constitute a tort. However, using an apparent 'best interests of the child' approach, the judge ruled that, although the Lebanese order was valid and subject to enforcement, it would be better for the daughter to remain with the defendant.

JOHN DOE I *et al*, Plaintiffs–Appellants v UNOCAL CORPORATION *et al*, Defendants–Appellees, 395 F3d 932 (2002) (*Doe v Unocal*)

This Ninth Circuit case reversed a lower court grant of summary judgment on an ATCA claim for forced labour, murder and rape, upheld a grant of summary judgment on claims of torture, and upheld the dismissal of claims against the state of Myanmar because of foreign sovereign immunity. The plaintiffs alleged that the defendants hired Myanmar military members to provide security on a major pipeline project, and with the knowledge of the defendants, these forces engaged in a campaign of forced labour, detaining local villagers, and under threat of force, making them work on the pipeline. Further, these forces continued their domination of the villagers by engaging in murder, rape and torture in order to secure their work or the work of others on the project. The court held that torture, murder, rape, forced labour, and slavery are *jus cogens* violations and 'thereby, violations of the law of nations'. State action is not required for claims of forced labour since it is a variation of slavery. Further, acts of murder, rape, and torture in furtherance of the forced labour programme are also proper subject-matter for an ATCA claim; however, there was insufficient evidence show the defendants had the necessary *mens rea* or *actus reus* for the alleged acts of torture.

VIETNAM ASSOCIATION FOR VICTIMS OF AGENT ORANGE *et al* v DOW CHEMICAL CO *et al*, 373 F Supp 2d 7 (2005)

In this Eastern District of New York case, the Court granted the defendants' motion to dismiss on all claims by the plaintiffs. The plaintiffs had alleged that defendants had manufactured a herbicide commonly known as Agent Orange for US military forces for use during the Vietnam conflict. US forces then used the herbicide in a manner that was dangerous to the plaintiffs, causing a host of injuries. The court dismissed all claims under domestic tort law, in part, because the defendants were acting under the direction of the government as government contractors. This government contractor defence did not apply, however, to claims of international tort. Using the holdings of *Filartiga* and *Karadžić* and tangentially the Supreme Court's holding in *Rasul v Bush*, the Court held that the claims under the ATCA were not non-justiciable political questions since they alleged violations of international law and the law of nations. The opinion respectfully cites this author's amicus brief submitted on behalf of the plaintiffs, but disagreed on his position that the use of Agent Orange constituted the use of poision in violation of the laws of war. This case has been upheld on appeal. The summary of the decision is contained in appendix two.

ALMOG *et al*, Plaintiffs v ARAB BANK, Defendant, 471 F Supp 2d 257 (*Almog v Arab Bank*)

The Eastern District of New York in this case denied the defendant's motion to dismiss ATCA claims by foreign nationals and certain claims under the Anti-Terrorism Act, but granted dismissal of claims under federal reporting requirements and certain federal common law claims. Over 1,600 plaintiffs alleged that the defendant aided and abetted suicide bomber terrorist attacks in Israel. Specifically the defendant 'knowingly and intentionally, both directly and indirectly, aided and abetted and intentionally facilitated the attacks by HAMAS, the PIJ, the AAMB, and the PFLP by soliciting, collecting, transmitting, disbursing and providing the financial resources that allowed those organizations to flourish and to engage in a campaign of terror, genocide, and crimes against humanity in an attempt to eradicate the Israeli presence from the Middle East landscape'. The plaintiffs stated that the defendant had bank accounts that served as a conduit of donations to the families of suicide bombers and as a collection point for terrorist organisations' fundraising efforts.

The court held that the alleged acts constituted acts of genocide and crimes against humanity and were thus cognisable violations of the law of nations under the ATCA using the *Sosa* test. Further, the Court found that the defendant's financial role could constitute aiding and abetting and thus find them complicitly liable for the terrorists' acts.

CYNTHIA CORRIE *et al*, Plaintiffs v CATERPILLAR, INC, Defendant, 403 F Supp 2d 1019 (2005)
(*Corrie v Caterpillar, Inc*)

In the Western District of Washington, the court dismissed all the plaintiff's claims, including those under the ATCA and international law. The plaintiff had alleged that the defendant manufactured and sold bulldozers to the Israeli Defense Force (IDF). This Force subsequently used them to destroy homes and conduct military attacks, one of which killed a family member of the plaintiff. In the ATCA portion of the opinion, the court used the *Sosa* test, focusing on the 'great caution' that courts should use before recognising new claims, to find that the alleged conduct did not constitute a violation of the law of nations under the ATCA. They further found that there was insufficient evidence that the defendant had aided and abetted the IDF in the alleged conduct. Finally, the court found that the plaintiffs were not aliens, and thus not able to bring a claim under the ATCA. This case has been affirmed on appeal. The summary of that decision is contained in appendix two.

SAKWE BALINTULO KHULUMANI *et al*, Plaintiffs–Appellants v BARCLAY NATIONAL BANK *et al*, Defendants–Appellees, 504 F.3d 254 (2007) (*Khulumani v Barclay National Bank*)

The Second Circuit vacated the lower court's dismissal of the plaintiffs' ATCA claim. The plaintiffs alleged that the approximately 50 corporate defendants 'actively and willingly collaborated with the government of South Africa in maintaining a repressive, racially based system known as "apartheid".' The lower court had granted the defendants' motion to dismiss under the ATCA, holding that there was no cognisable claim for aider and abettor liability under the law of nations. The dismissal was vacated and the case remanded.

APPENDIX TWO

Additional ATCA-related Cases not Cited in the Text

RICARDO A DE LOS SANTOS MORA, Plaintiff–Appellant v THE PEOPLE OF THE STATE OF NEW YORK, RICHARD A BROWN, District Att, FLUSHING QUEENS POLICE DEPT, Defendants–Appellees, 524 F3d 183 (2008) (*De los Santos Mora v New York*)

When the plaintiff was held by police officers, they did not notify him that, under Article 36 of the Vienna Convention on Consular Relations, he had the right to notify the local consulate of his detention. The district court dismissed the ATCA claim, and the Second Circuit affirmed, holding that, although the US authorities had an obligation to notify the local consulate in accordance with Article 36, failure to do so did not create an individual right of action. Using the 'vigilant doorkeeper' approach espoused by *Sosa*, the view prevailed that the violation of Article 36 consular notification of detention was not defined with a specificity comparable to the features of the eighteenth-century paradigms.

JACOB AIKPITANHI *et al*, Plaintiffs v IBERIA AIRLINES OF SPAIN, Defendant, 553 F Supp 2d 872 (2008) (*Aikpitanhi v Iberia Airlines of Spain*)

The plaintiffs alleged that, as a result of tortious activity, their father was killed on a flight with defendant airline between Nigeria and Spain while in the custody of Spanish officials. The defendant argued that the sole source of jurisdiction for an incident on an aircraft was the Montreal Convention (Convention for the Unification of Certain Rules for International Carriage by Air, May 28, 1999), thus preventing jurisdiction under the ATCA. The district court agreed and dismissed.

BINYAM MOHAMED *et al*, **Plaintiffs v JEPPESEN DATAPLAN, Inc, Defendant, 539 F Supp 2d 1128** (*Mohamed v Dataplan*)

The plaintiffs alleged that they were the victims of extraordinary rendition, a Central Intelligence Agency programme in which they were 'unlawfully apprehended, transported, imprisoned, interrogated and in some instances tortured'. The government moved to intervene on behalf of itself and the defendant, claiming that the subject-matter of the case involved state secrets. The court granted the government's assertion of the state secret privilege and right to intervene, but was careful to note that their ruling did not state that the cause of action lacked subject-matter jurisdiction under the ATCA.

VIET NAM ASSOCIATION FOR VICTIMS OF AGENT ORANGE *et al* v **DOW CHEMICAL CO** *et al*, **517 F3d 104 (2008)**

This is an affirmation of the 2005 case cited in appendix one. The Second Circuit upheld the lower court dismissal for failure to state a claim under the ATCA. The Court cited the executive and legislative history to the signing of the 1925 Geneva Gas Protocol that the US did not consider the use of herbicide defoliates to be covered by the protocol. Stating that there was a lack of consensus in the international community, the Court ruled that the use of herbicides as a defoliate failed to meet the *Sosa* test and was therefore not an actionable violation of the law of nations. The plaintiffs also alleged that the use of herbicides violated the customary law of war norms of proportionality and unnecessary suffering; however, the Court held that violations of these norms required a higher level of intent ('willfully', 'calculated to cause', or 'carried out unlawfully or wantonly') that was not met by the allegation in this case.

ANTONIO GONZALEZ CARRIZOSA *et al*, **Plaintiffs v CHIQUITA BRANDS INTERNATIONAL, INC** *et al*, **Defendants, 2007 US Dist LEXIS 84308 (2007)** (*Carrizosa v Chiquita*)

In this novel case filed in the Southern District of Florida, the plaintiffs sued a major US corporation for the consequences of terrorist acts, committed by an organisation which made payments making payments to an organisation identified by the United States as a terrorist fundraiser. The payments themselves were determined to be illegal. The plaintiffs are pursuing tort action for damages from terrorist attacks funded by this operation. The cited case, the only published record to date, merely denies the defence motion for change of venue.

PRINCE ALBERT CZETWERTYNSKI, Plaintiff v UNITED STATES OF AMERICA *et al*, US Ambassador to Poland, Defendants, 514 F Supp 2d 592 (2007) (*Czetwertynski v United States*)

The Southern District of New York dismissed the plaintiff's claim to damages under the ATCA. The plaintiff, the Prince of Poland, lost rights to certain property in Poland with the onset of the communist regime there. The United States subsequently rented some of this property from the new Polish government to be used as an embassy and destroyed the buildings thereon in order to build the embassy. The plaintiff is suing for damages from the destroyed buildings. The Court found that the ATCA did not contain a waiver of sovereign immunity by the United States, specifically finding that the Federal Tort Claims Act did not include such a waiver (as it did in *Sosa*) for the facts at bar.

JOHN ROE I *et al*, Plaintiffs v BRIDGESTONE CORPORATION *et al*, Defendants, 492 F Supp 2d 988 (2007) (*Roe v Bridgestone*)

The Southern District of Indiana dismissed most of the plaintiffs' claims under the ATCA, but denied dismissal of a child labour claim. The plaintiffs alleged that they were forced to work under horrible conditions. Although the coercion to work was not directly applied by the defendants, if the plaintiffs did not work extensive hours in poor conditions, their only option, allegedly, was to quit and starve in a nation with over 80 per cent unemployment. The plaintiffs also alleged that the minimum work requirement each day mandated that they use their minor children as assistants in the task and that the defendants encouraged this practice. The Court found that the concept of 'forced labour' as a violation of the law of nations developed in case law did not apply to the facts alleged by the plaintiffs. The Court made special notice that the plaintiffs used aliases in their complaint for the express purpose of protecting their identities to prevent losing the jobs they were alleged to have been forced into. Finding that the complaint alleged that the defendants knowingly employed seven-, eight- and ten-year-old children who worked with harmful chemicals, the Court ruled that this allegation, if proven, would violate the law of nations as oppressive child labour and thus allowed this portion of the complaint to stand.

CYNTHIA CORRIE *et al*, Plaintiffs v CATERPILLAR INC, Defendant, 503 F3d 974 (2007) (*Corrie v Caterpillar, Inc*)

This case affirms the district court decision discussed in appendix one. The Ninth Circuit held, on the basis of political questions, that the Court should jurisdiction over the matter. Noting that the bull-dozers the defendant used in the alleged destruction of homes were in fact paid for by the executive branch of the US Government, the Court held that allowing the action to proceed would require the judicial branch to question 'the political branch's decision to grant extensive military aid to Israel'. They ruled that the cause of action was a non-justiciable political question and that it was 'not the role of the courts to indirectly indict Israel for violating international law with military equipment the United States government provided and continues to provide'.

ALEXIS HOLYWEEK SAREI *et al*, Plaintiffs–Appellees v RIO TINTO *et al*, Defendants–Appellants, 499 F3d 923 (2007) (*Sarei v Rio Tinto*)

The Ninth Circuit reversed and vacated the lower court's dismissal on political question, act of state, and comity grounds. The plain-tiffs alleged that the defendant, a mining company headquartered in London, asked the military forces of Papua New Guinea (PNG_ to commit 'atrocious human rights abuses and war crimes … including blockade, aerial bombardment of civilian targets, burning of villages, rape and pillage', in order to keep its mining operations open on the island of Bougainville. The district court had ruled that the allegations were proper subject-matter for an ATCA claim, but that they involved non-justiciable political questions, acts of foreign sovereigns, and would violate international comity grounds. Holding that the war crimes were not frivolous allegations of a violation of the law of nations, the appellate court ruled that ATCA jurisdiction was proper. They further supported this ruling by finding that federal common law had 'well-settled' theories of vicarious liability allowing the plaintiffs' claims against the defendant to proceed.

HAFSAT ABIOLA *et al*, Plaintiffs v ABDULSALAMI ABUBAKAR, Defendant, 2007 US Dist LEXIS 20311 (2007) (*Abiola v Abubakar*)

This Northern District of Illinois opinion marked the final dispute in a prolonged litigation process concerning primarily service of process, personal jurisdiction, and default judgment disputes that concluded in an out-of-court settlement. The plaintiffs alleged that the defendant, a member of a military regime that ruled Nigeria from 1993 to 1999, tortured either the plaintiffs or their parents for publicly questioning the regime. The court found subject-matter jurisdiction in the Torture Victim Protection Act.

JOGI v VOGES *et al*, 480 F3d 833 (2007) (*Jogi II*)

In this Seventh Circuit Court of Appeals case, the Court avoided deciding if failure to notify a foreign national of his right to consular notification under Article 36 of the Vienna Convention on Consular Relations would constitute a 'tort' and a valid cause of action under the ATCA. Instead the Court found that the alleged conduct was clearly within the General Federal Jurisdiction Statute, 28 USC 1331.

ROMIL RAFAEL ESTRELLA TAVERAS, Plaintiff–Appellant v CAROLYN R PAIEWONSKY TAVERAZ, Defendant–Appellee, 477 F3d 767 (2007) (*Tavaras v Tavaraz*)

In this Sixth Circuit case, the Court affirmed a lower court dismissal of a claim of parental child abduction. The alleged facts were that the defendant mother had taken two children from the plaintiff father by moving them from the Dominican Republic to the United States on a tourist visa and then stating an intent never to return to the Dominican Republic. The plaintiff alleged that defendant's fraudulent entry into the United States on a tourist visa despite having an intent to remain there permanently constituted a violation of the international law of safe conduct and thus gave rise to a cause of action under the ATCA. The Court held that the plaintiff's interpretation of the law of safe conduct was incorrect and rejected the plaintiff's other claims.

LARRY BOWOTO *et al*, Plaintiffs v CHEVRON CORPORATION *et al*, Defendants, 2007 US Dist LEXIS 59374 (2007) (*Bowoto v Chevron*)

In this Northern District of California case, the court recognised allegations of 'crimes against humanity' as actionable under the ATCA, but, however, granted the defence motion for summary judgment because the plaintiffs failed to meet the pleading require-ments to allege a crime against humanity. The plaintiffs alleged that when they protested against an offshore oil platform in 1998, the defendants, through their Nigerian subsidiary, responded by attacking and killing the protestors both on the platform and the following day at their respective villages, burning them to the ground.

The court analysed the Rome Statute on crimes against human-ity, separating it into three components:

1. the conditions of the crime, namely a widespread or systematic attack directed against any civilian population;
2. one of the specific crimes listed, such as murder or rape or tor-ture; and
3. a connection between the conditions of the crime and the crime committed.

The court ruled that, although there was factual evidence of attacks on oil protestors, the plaintiffs had not alleged facts that would support a finding that these attacks were a widespread or systemic attack against a civilian population.

CARMEN T CISNEROS, Plaintiff–Appellant v MICHAEL J ARAGON, Defendant–Appellee, 485 F3d 1236 (2007) (*Cisneros v Aragon*)

In this Tenth Circuit case, the court dismissed a then minor victim's allegations of sexual abuse, finding that these acts did not constitute a tort in violation of the law of nations. The plaintiff alleged that at the age of 15 she was forced into marriage with the defendant, who proceeded both to rape and to statutorily rape her and commit sexual acts upon her person when she was incapable of consent. The court ruled that although these acts may be criminalised by US law, this is not conclusive evidence that they are torts that violate the law of nations.

Using the *Sosa* 'vigilant doorkeeper' approach, the court found insufficient evidence that these alleged sexual acts under the facts alleged rose to the level of violating an international norm.

MOSHE SAPERSTEIN *et al*, Plaintiffs v THE PALESTINIAN AUTHORITY, THE PALESTINE LIBERATION ORGANIZATION, *et al*, Defendants, 2006 US Dist LEXIS 92778 (2006) (*Saperstein v The Palestinion Authority*)

In this Southern District of Florida case, the court dismissed the plaintiffs' claims for recovery under the ATCA due to terrorist attacks. Citing the Edwards opinion from *Tel-Oren*, the court held that politically motivated terrorism has not risen to the level of a violation of the law of nations.

JUAN ROMAGOZA ARCE *et al*, Plaintiffs–Appellees v JOSE GUILLERMO GARCIA *et al*, Defendants–Appellants, 434 F3d 1254 (2006) (*Arce v Garcia*)

The Eleventh Circuit affirmed the lower court denial of the defendants' motion to dismiss based on the statute of limitations. The plaintiffs alleged that they were subject to torture by the Salvadorean military from 1979 to 1983. The defence argued that they failed to file suit in the Torture Victim Protection Act within the ten-year statute of limitations. The Court denied the motion based upon equitable tolling, finding that the plaintiffs reasonably delayed filing until the end of the civil war in 1992 because they feared reprisals against family members still in El Salvador.

ANGEL ENRIQUE VILLEDA ALDANA *et al*, Plaintiffs–Appellants v FRESH DEL MONTE PRODUCE *et al*, Defendants–Appellees, 452 F3d 1284 (2006)
(*Angel v Del Monte*)

In this Eleventh Circuit Court of Appeals case, the court, in a one-paragraph opinion, denied a suggestion of rehearing en banc. Judge Barkett, in a lengthy dissent, argued that this decision was not in accordance with the analysis established by *Sosa*. Arguing that the majority had determined that 'cruel, inhuman or degrading treatment or punishment' could not give rise to an ATCA cause of action, Judge Barkett labelled the opinion 'precedent-setting error of exceptional importance'. When looking at the sources suggested by *Sosa*—treaties, judicial decisions, the practice of governments, and the opinions of international law scholars—Judge Barkett found a 'universal, definable, and obligatory prohibition against the cruel, inhuman, or degrading treatment or punishment' and determined it was actionable under the ATCA.

URSULA UNGARO-BENAGES, Plaintiff–Appellant v DRESDNER BANK AG, DEUTSCHE BANK AG, Defendants–Appellees, 379 F3d 1227 (2004) (*Ungaro-Benages v Dresdner Bank*)

In this Eleventh Circuit case, the Court found an ATCA complaint to be justiciable despite a State Department statement of interest claiming that the case concerned a political question. The plaintiff alleged that the defendants had 'Aryanised' certain stock possessions in the modern-day Fiat Corporation from the estate of her grandparents. The State Department submitted a statement of interest claiming that allowing this case to proceed would disrupt the Foundation 'Remembrance, Responsibility and the Future'

Agreement between the United States and Germany. The Court held this insufficient to justify dismissal on political question grounds, but ruled that the Foundation provided an adequate remedy for the plaintiff and dismissed on grounds of international comity.

HOANG VAN TU *et al*, Plaintiffs–Appellants v MAJOR GENERAL KOSTER *et al*, Defendants–Appellees, 364 F3d 1196 (2004)

In this Tenth Circuit case, the Court was forced to dismiss the claims of the victims of the famous My Lai massacre during the Vietnam conflict. The Court ruled that the plaintiffs violated the ten-year statute of limitations under the Torture Victim Protection Act.

JANE DOE I *et al*, Plaintiffs v LAKIREDDY BALI REDDY *et al*, Defendants, 2003 US Dist LEXIS 26120 (2003) (*Doe v Reddy*)

In this Northern District of California case, the court denied a motion to dismiss a claim under the ATCA. The allegations were that the defendants fraudulently induced the plaintiffs, a group of young women, to come to the United States with promises of education and employment. Upon arrival they were forced into jobs with long hours under arduous conditions at illegally low wages, and in the course of which they were sexually abused, beaten, and threatened. The court ruled that these allegations supported actionable causes of action for forced labour, debt bondage, and trafficking under the ATCA.

RAPHAEL BIGIO, BAHIA BIGIO, FERIAL SALMA BIGIO and B BIGIO & CO, Plaintiffs–Appellants v THE COCA-COLA COMPANY and THE COCA-COLA EXPORT COMPANY, Defendants–Appellees, 239 F3d 440 (2000) (*Bigio v Coca-Cola*)

In this Second Circuit case, the Court upheld the lower court's dismissal of claims under the ATCA, though reversing and remanding under diversity jurisdiction. The plaintiffs alleged that in 1960 the government of Egypt nationalised their factories and plants in Heliopolis, Egypt, because of their Jewish status. The defendant subsequently (1993) bought and leased parts of this property knowing that it had been illegally seized. The Court ruled that the plaintiffs had failed to allege a violation of the law of nations. Although the seizure may have been illegal, the defendant was not operating in conspiracy with the Egyptian government or 'under the color of law'.

ELSA IWANOWA *et al*, Plaintiffs v FORD MOTOR COMPANY and FORD WERKE AG, Defendants, 67 F Supp 2d 424 (1999) (*Iwanowa v Ford*)

The District Court of New Jersey dismissed all claims unrelated to the ATCA but identified that allegations of forced labour, as established by the Nuremburg Tribunals, violate customary international law. The plaintiff alleged that she was sold from her home in Russia and sent to Germany where she was forced to work for the German subsidiary of Ford. Although only 17, she was housed in a wooden hut without any heat or facilities, forced to perform heavy labour, and beaten when she failed to meet quotas. The case was dismissed as time-barred and because it raised non-justiciable political questions.

TOM BEANAL *et al*, Plaintiff–Appellant v FREEPORT-MCMORAN, INC, AND FREEPORT MCMORAN COPPER AND GOLD, INC, Defendants–Appellees, 197 F3d 161 (1999) (*Beanal v Freeport McMoran, Inc*)

In this Fifth Circuit case, the Court ruled that the plaintiff failed to provide enough detail to constitute a complaint of violation of the law of nations. The plaintiff alleged that the defendant, while operating a mining operation in Indonesia, engaged in: (1) individual human rights violations; (2) environmental torts; and (3) genocide and cultural genocide. The Court held that the claim of individual rights violations lacked the necessary specificity for a federal complaint. The plaintiff did not allege any specific wrong doing to himself, but rather acts against others for which he had no standing.

HIRUTE ABEBE-JIRA *et al*, Plaintiffs–Appellees v KELBESSA NEGEWO, Defendant–Appellant, 72 F3d 844, (1996) (*Abebe-Jira v Negewo*)

In this Eleventh Circuit case, the Court upheld a decision to award damages under the ATCA for torture and cruel, inhuman treatment. The district court found that the defendant, acting in an official capacity for a military dictatorship in Ethiopia, engaged in beating, humiliating, and torturing the plaintiffs and their family members. The defendant moved to set aside the verdict and dismiss for lack of subject-matter jurisdiction. Specifically, the defendant argued that the ATCA did not provide for a private right of action. Citing international law conventions and human rights treaties, the court ruled that torture and cruel, inhuman, or degrading treatment or punishment is actionable under the ATCA as a violation of the law of nations. Further, they found that 'Congress, therefore, has recognized that the Alien Tort Claims Act confers both a forum and a private right of action to aliens alleging a violation of international law'.

IN RE ESTATE OF FERDINAND MARCOS, HUMAN RIGHTS LITIGATION. MAXIMO HILAO, *et al*, Class Plaintiffs, Plaintiffs–Appellees, v ESTATE OF FERDINAND MARCOS, Defendant–Appellant, 25 F3d 1467 (1994) (*Marcos III*)

In this famous Ninth Circuit class action, (See also *Marcos I*, 978 F2d 493) the Court affirmed the lower court decision allowing the case to proceed, finding that the action was not barred by the Foreign Sovereign Immunities Act (FSIA). The plaintiffs alleged that during the tenure of Ferdinand Marcos as the President of the Philippines, over 10,000 members of the class or their relatives were tortured, summarily executed, or disappeared at the hands of military forces under the control and direction of Marcos. The defendant argued that these claims had abated with Marcos's death, were barred by the FSIA, or did not give rise to a cause of action under the ATCA. The Court determined that torture violated a *jus cogens* norm and was therefore a violation of the law of nations and that the ATCA was not purely a jurisdictional statute. Federal subject-matter jurisdiction could still be applied even when it was determined that the FSIA was inapplicable. The ATCA did not contain the requirement that causes of action 'arise under' the laws of the United States. The Court held that since the alleged acts were not taken within any official mandate, they were not acts of a foreign state under the FSIA so that Act was inapplicable.

GOLDSTAR (PANAMA) SA *et al*, Plaintiffs–Appellants v UNITED STATES, Defendant–Appellee, 967 F2d 965 (1992) (*Goldstar (Panama) SA v United States*)

In this Fourth Circuit case, the Court dismissed claims by Panamanian businesses for damage during the post-Noriega invasion period. The plaintiffs alleged that US forces violated the terms of the Hague Convention when, after invading and toppling the Noriega government in Panama, they failed to perform their duties as an occupying force. Specifically, they failed to restore and maintain public order, resulting in damages from looting and other such activities directed against the plaintiffs' businesses. The Court held that the Hague Convention was not self-executing and did not create a cause of action/waiver of sovereign immunity under the ATCA, and the discretionary function exception to the FTCA barred action under that statute.

ARGENTINE REPUBLIC v AMERADA HESS SHIPPING CORP *et al* 488 US 428 (1988)

The Supreme Court overturned the Second Circuit and reinstated the district court's dismissal of the case. The plaintiffs allege that the defendants destroyed their oil tanker, a non-combatant non-belligerent ship during the Falklands/Malvinas war, and that the manner of the attack violated international law. The plaintiffs sued in tort under the ATCA. The Court found, however, that the only source of jurisdiction over a foreign sovereign must come under the FSIA, and that the plaintiff failed to allege a justiciable cause of action under this statute.

KEITH CARMICHAEL *et al*, Plaintiffs–Appellants v UNITED TECHNOLOGIES CORP *et al*, Defendants–Appellees, 835 F2d 109 (1988) (*Carmichael v United Technologies*)

In this Fifth Circuit case, the Court dismissed the plaintiffs' claim due to lack of subject-matter jurisdiction. The plaintiff alleged that he was held in a Saudi prison for two years and tortured at the behest of the defendants. There was a credit dispute between the parties and when the plaintiff attempted to flee Saudi Arabia without his passport, he was captured and held in prison until all claims against him were released by his creditors, which included the defendants. The plaintiff alleges that the defendants delayed signing a release in order to take advantage of the coercive effect of the Saudi prison in inducing the plaintiff to waive his rights in a counter-claim against the defendants. The Court ruled that even if torture violated the law of nations, there was no evidence that the defendants had any role in the alleged torture. The defendants did not ask for or aid/abet the plaintiff's arrest and incarceration, and they had no legal responsibility to waive a valid claim of debt against him in order to secure his release.

MC ZAPATA, Plaintiff–Appellant v JOHN D QUINN, Director, New York State Lottery, and THE STATE OF NEW YORK, by Robert Abrams, Attorney General, Defendants-Appellees, 707 F2d 691 (1983) (*Zapata v Quinn*)

In this Second Circuit case, the Court refined the standard for alleging violations of the law of nations under the ATCA in accordance with *Filartiga*. Specifically, only law of nations violations that are 'shockingly egregious violations of universally recognized principles of international law' can support a claim under the ATCA. The plaintiff alleged deprivation of property when she received only a portion of her lottery winnings immediately, with the rest in the form of an annual annuity. The Court dismissed her complaint, labelling it frivolous.

BOLCHOS v DARREL, 1795 US Dist 4, 3 F Cas 810 (1795)

In this first reported case of ATCA application, the district court ruled that it had jurisdiction over the matter under that statute. The plaintiff, who had lawfully captured a Spanish ship (prize) filled with slaves, docked in the United States. The defendant seized the slaves upon docking and sold them to repay the debts incurred by their prior Spanish owner. The court ruled that the slaves were the lawful property of the plaintiff, despite their neutral status, based on the stowage on an enemy ship. He ordered the proceeds of their sale to be paid to the plaintiff.

Index